General Knowledge

(Indian & World Geography)

Compiled & Edited
Research & Editorial Deptt.

V&S PUBLISHERS

Published by:

V&S PUBLISHERS

F-2/16, Ansari road, Daryaganj, New Delhi-110002
☎ 23240026, 23240027 • *Fax:* 011-23240028
Email: info@vspublishers.com • *Website:* www.vspublishers.com

Regional Office : Hyderabad
5-1-707/1, Brij Bhawan (Beside Central Bank of India Lane)
Bank Street, Koti, Hyderabad - 500 095
☎ 040-24737290
E-mail: vspublishershyd@gmail.com

Branch Office : Mumbai
Jaywant Industrial Estate, 1st Floor–108, Tardeo Road
Opposite Sobo Central Mall, Mumbai – 400 034
☎ 022-23510736
E-mail: vspublishersmum@gmail.com

Follow us on:

DISCLAIMER

While every attempt has been made to provide accurate and timely information in this book, neither the author nor the publisher assumes any responsibility for errors, unintended omissions or commissions detected therein. The author and publisher make no representation or warranty with respect to the comprehensiveness or completeness of the contents provided.

All matters included have been simplified under professional guidance for general information only without any warranty for applicability on an individual. Any mention of an organization or a website in the book by way of citation or as a source of additional information doesn't imply the endorsement of the content either by the author or the publisher. It is possible that websites cited may have changed or removed between the time of editing and publishing the book.

Results from using the expert opinion in this book will be totally dependent on individual circumstances and factors beyond the control of the author and the publisher.

It makes sense to elicit advice from well informed sources before implementing the ideas given in the book. The reader assumes full responsibility for the consequences arising out from reading this book. For proper guidance, it is advisable to read the book under the watchful eyes of parents/guardian. The purchaser of this book assumes all responsibility for the use of given materials and information. The copyright of the entire content of this book rests with the author/publisher. Any infringement/ transmission of the cover design, text or illustrations, in any form, by any means, by any entity will invite legal action and be responsible for consequences thereon.

Printed at Repro Knowledgecast Limited, Thane

PUBLISHER'S NOTE

V&S Publishers is constant in its effort to identify the problems faced by the aspirants of various competitive examinations held at state and national levels, and to sort out those problems effectively. After a thorough search in the market, we realised that there are a few books available on comprehensive General Knowledge, which are too costly and too large to go through in short span of time during preparation. The present book, **'General Knowledge'** with all genres of general awareness has been designed to meet the specific needs of the contestants of various entrance exams and competitive exams as well. Not only does the book spreads awareness, but also can be a facilitator of change in life.

The book has been strategically planned in order to be user friendly. It covers up-to-date knowledge on *Geography (India and World)*. The primary goal is to fulfil the quest for knowledge on various topics of study at national and international levels.

The book is recommended for various competitive examinations such as:

- Civil Services
- Staff Selection Commission (SSC)
- Institute of Banking Personnel Selection (IBPS)
- Defence Services – CDSE, NDA and other defence services
- Management Aptitude Test (MAT), Common Admission Test (CAT), and Graduate Management Admission Test (GMAT)
- Indian Engineering Services
- Railway Recruitment Services
- Test of English as a Foreign Language (TOEFL)
- International English Language Testing System (IELTS)

We hope that the book will be of immense help to the readers to up-grade their knowledge on various topics of general knowledge. A regular revision of all the topics covered in the book is advised to get up-to-date with the required information. We wish all aspirants good luck for their future endeavours.

CONTENTS

GEOGRAPHY

World Geography

1. The Universe

The universe is the term used collectively for all that exists physically – Space, planets, galaxies and all forms of matter and energy. Its age is estimated at **13 billion years**. The universe contains galaxies which developed 12 billion years ago. These galaxies are made up of **stars**, alongwith **gas** and **dust**. All of this is held together by gravity. There are three kinds of galaxies – *elliptical, spiral* and *irregular*. The galaxy that contains the earth's solar system is called the **Milky Way**. It is a spiral galaxy which can be seen in the night sky as a broad band of faint light.

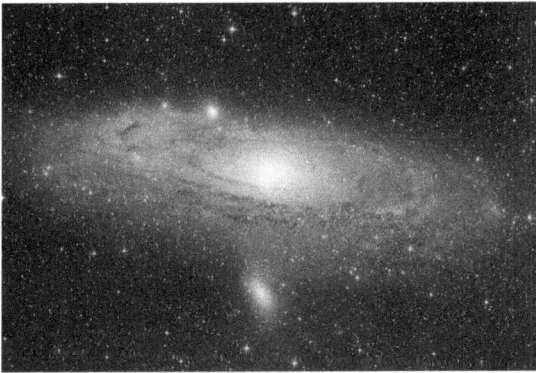

The outer space is that region of space that lies beyond the Earth's atmosphere. It can be measured using Light Year and Astronomical Unit (AU). A Light year is the distance that light can travel in one year. An Astronomical Unit is the average distance between the Sun and the Earth. One light-year is equal to 9,500,000,000,000 kilometres and One AU would be 1,49,597,870 kilometres.

The study of the universe is called **Cosmology**. **Astronomy** is the study of the sun, the planets, the moon and all other celestial bodies of the universe.

A star is a ball of hydrogen and helium gas. Its core is extremely hot and dense. There are millions of stars, the sun being one of the major one. It is less than one light year away from the earth. Stars make up about 98 percent of a galaxy, while the other 2 percent is made up of gas and dust. Other important stars are *Proxima Centauri, Alpha Centauri,* etc. *Red Giants* are stars which have a low surface temperature. When their hydrogen content lessens, their outer region grows and reddens, therefore their name. The star begins to die in this stage. The sun is expected to become a red giant in about 5 billion years.

Supernova and **Nova** are stars that have a sudden increase in brightness, which fades back to normal after a while. This occurs due to a sudden partial or complete explosion. In Nova, the star's outer shell explodes and in Supernova, it is the whole star which explodes. **Pulsars** are stars which discharge *electromagnetic waves*.

A **black hole** is a dense region of space which has the ability to swallow up everything, even light. It has a very strong gravitational field. The term, 'black hole' was coined by **John Wheeler**, an US physicist in 1967.

2. The Solar System

The system that contains the Sun and the Earth and its neighbouring planets is called the Solar System. They are held together by the gravitational pull of the Sun. The Sun and planets were formed out of the Nebula which was a giant cloud of gas and dust. It was after this cloud collapsed that the formation of the Earth took place approximately 4.5 billion years ago.

Structure of the Solar System

About 99.85 percent of the total mass of the Solar System is contained in the Sun. The planets contain only 0.135 percent of the matter, while the remaining 0.015 percent is contained in natural *satellites, meteoroids, comets, asteroids*, etc.

The Sun

The Sun is the star closest to the earth and it lies at the centre of the solar system. Its age is approximately *5 billion years old*. Its diametre is around 1,384,000 km and its mass is 3,30,000, more than that of the Earth. It consists mainly of Hydrogen (71%) and Helium (26.5%). There are other elements which constitute about 2.5 percent.

The Sun revolves in a circular orbit around the galaxy's centre at a speed of 250 km/s. The period taken by the Sun to complete one revolution around the galactic centre is called a **cosmic year**. The Sun takes 250 million years to do this.

The Sun lies at a distance of 149.8 million km from the earth. Measured in light years, the distance is less than one light year. Its light takes approximately **8.3 minutes** to reach the earth.

Parts of the Sun

⇨ **Photosphere**- It is the glowing surface of the Sun. It is about 400 km thick and its temperature varies from 4226°C to 5276°C.

⇨ **Chromosphere**- It is the part which contains gases that develop from the photosphere. It is about 10,000 km thick and temperatures range from 4226°C to 9726°C.

⇨ **Corona**- It is the outermost region of the Sun. It is made up of a sequence of colours- Violet, Indigo, Blue, Green, Yellow, Orange and Red (VIBGYOR). The corona can be seen during a Solar Eclipse.

Other Elements

⇨ **Plages**- Bright spots on the surface of the Sun.

⇨ **Sunspots**- Dark spots on the surface of the Sun.

The sun gets energy from the *nuclear fissions* that take place in its interior. It uses *four million tonnes of hydrogen per second.*

Planets

Our solar system contains *eight planets*- Mercury, Venus, Earth, Mars, Jupiter, Saturn, Uranus and Neptune. *Jupiter is the largest planet in terms of size*, followed by Saturn, Uranus, Neptune, Earth, Venus, Mars and Mercury.

Pluto was considered the *ninth planet from 1930 to 2006*. But in 2006, an official definition for the term, 'planet' was created by the International Astronomical Union (IAU), and under this Pluto was categorised as a 'dwarf planet'. *All planets except Uranus have a perpendicular axis of rotation. Uranus also has an elliptical axis.*

Planet	Mean Distance from the Sun (km)	Diametre (km)	Diametre Relative to the Earth	Time to Orbit the Sun (Years)
Mercury	58 10^6	4,880	0.38	0.24
Venus	108 10^6	12,100	0.95	0.62
Earth	150 10^6	12,760	1.00	1.00
Mars	228 10^6	6,800	0.53	1.88
Jupiter	778 10^6	143,800	11.27	11.86
Saturn	1,427 10^6	120,000	9.44	29.46
Uranus	2,870 10^6	52,300	4.10	84.01
Neptune	4,497 10^6	49,500	3.88	164.79
Pluto (dwarf planet)	5,900 10^6	3,000	0.20	247.7

Asteroids are small, rocky elements that are too small to be called planets. They are usually fragments of planets which can be found between the orbits of Mars and Jupiter. They are also known as *planetoids or minor planets*. **Ceres** was the largest asteroid, but recently it was categorised as a *dwarf planet*.

Meteors or more commonly called *shooting stars*, are pieces of debris. They can be as small as a grain of sand or as huge as a boulder. They burn up due to friction in the atmosphere. Meteorites are those which burn and fall onto the earth's surface.

Comets are made up of ice, dust, carbon dioxide, ammonia, methane, etc. They orbit around the Sun and release gas and dust. **Halley's Comet** is one of the most famous comets. It last appeared in 1986 and will appear next in mid-2061.

The *Moon* is the *earth's only natural satellite*. It lies at a distance of about 3, 82,200 km from the earth and is about one-sixth its size. The moon takes *27 days, 7 hours and 43 minutes* to complete one revolution around the earth.

The first human mission to the moon took place on July 21, 1967. **Neil Armstrong** and **Edwin Aldrin** were the first people to set foot on the moon.

3. Continents of The World

Asia, Africa, North America, South America, Europe, Australia and Antarctica are the seven continents.

Facts about Asia

Latitude	:	10°S and 80°N
Longitude	:	25°E and 170°W
Area	:	44,579,000 sq. km. (approx 30% of the world)
Population	:	3,879 million (est. 2008) .
Oceans and Seas	:	Arctic Ocean, Pacific Ocean, Indian Ocean, Red Sea, Gulf of Aden, Persian Gulf, Gulf of Oman, Arabian Sea, Bay of Bengal, China Sea, Yellow Sea of Okhotsk, Bering Sea.
Highest and Lowest Points	:	Everest (8,848 metres) and Dead Sea (–396.8 m) respectively.
Straits	:	Strait of Malacca, Bering Strait.
Lakes	:	Caspian Sea, Aral Sea, Lake Baikal, Lake Balkhash.
Islands	:	Kurile, Sakhalin, Honshu, Hokkaido, Taiwan, Borneo, Sumatra, Java, Celebes, New Guinea, Philippines, Sri Lanka, Bahrain, Cyprus.
Mountains	:	Pamir Knot, Himalayas, Karakoram, Kunlun, Tien Shan, Altai, Hindu kush, Elbruz, Pontic, Sulaiman, Zagros, Taurus, Urals, Yablonovoi, Stanovoi.

Plateaus	:	Anatolia Plateau, Plateau of Iran, Plateau of Arabia, Plateau of Tibet, Tarim Basin, Plateau of Mongolia, Plateau of Yunnan, Decan Plateau.
Peninsulas	:	Kamchatka Peninsula, Peninsula of Korea, Peninsula of Indo-China, Malay Peninsula, Indian Peninsula, Arabian Peninsula.
Deserts	:	Arabian Desert, Thar Desert, Gobi Desert.
Rivers	:	Eupharates, Tigris, Indus, Ganga, Brahmaputra, Hwang-Ho, Yang-tse, Si-kiang, Amur, Lena Yenisei, Ob, Irrawady, Salween, Mekong.
Important Cities	:	Aden, Karachi, New Delhi, Mumbai, Kolkata, Colombo, Yangon (former Rangoon), Kuala Lumpur, Bangkok, Ho Chi Minh City (former Saigon), Singapore, Manila, Guangzhou (former Canton), Hong Kong, Shanghai, Tokyo.

Facts about Africa

Latitude	:	35°S and 37°N
Longitude	:	50°E and 17°W
Population	:	1,000,050,000 (2009 est.)
Area	:	30,065,000 sq. km (approx.) (20.4% of the world).
Oceans and Seas	:	Indian Ocean, Red Sea, Atlantic Ocean, Gulf of Guinea, Mediterranean Sea.
Highest and Lowest Points	:	Kilimanjaro (5,895 m.) and Lake Assai (−156.1 m.) respectively.
Straits	:	Strait of Bab-el-Mandeb, Straits of Gibraltar.
Lakes	:	Victoria, Tanganyka, Malawi, Chad, Rudolf, Albert.
Islands	:	Madagascar, Cape Verde Islands, The Comoros, Mauritius, Seychelles.
Mountains	:	Atlas, Drakensberg, Kilimanjaro.
Plateaus	:	Plateau of Africa – the entire continent is a plateau.
Deserts	:	Sahara, Kalahari, Namib.

Facts about North America

North America, northern continent of Western Hemisphere, comprising U.S.A., Canada, Central America and the Caribbean, on west high chain of mountains, lower range in east and central plains. Climate varies considerably owing to wide range of latitude and altitude.

Latitude	: 7°N and 84°N
Longitude	: 20°W and 180°W
Area	: 24,235,280 sq. km (approx.) (16.3%).
Population	: 528,720,588 (est. 2008).
Major Deserts	: Chihuahuan, Colorado, Mujave, Sonoran.
Major Lakes	: Lake Superior (largest sweet water lake in the world), Huron, Michigan, Great Slave, Great Bear, Erie, Ontario, etc.
Major Rivers	: Mississippi, Missourie, St. Lawrence, Mackenzie, Colorado, Hudson, Potomac, Ohio etc.
Oceans and Seas	: Atlantic Ocean, Pacific Ocean, Arctic Ocean, Gulf of Mexico, Caribbean Sea, Gulf of California, Gulf of Alska, Bering Sea, Hudson Bay.
Highest and Lowest Points	: Mckinley (6,194 m.) and Death Valley (–85.9 m.) respectively.
Straits	: Bering Strait.
Islands	: Greenland, Baffin, Victoria, New foundland, Cuba, Jamaica, Haiti.
Mountains	: Rockies, Appalachain, Brooks, Kuskolkwim, Alaska Range, Cascade Range, Coastal Range, Sierra Nevada, Sierra Madre etc.
Plateaus	: Columbia Plateau, Colorado Plateau, Mexican Plateau, Canadian Shield.
Agriculture	: Temperate and tropical products, cereals, tobacco, sugarbeet, potatoes etc.
Minerals	: Coal, petroleum, iron, manganese etc.
Industries	: Ship building, occupied formerly by Red Indians; now mainly by Whites with many Blacks in the south.
Important cities	: New York, Washington D.C., Boston, Chicago, Dallas, Detroit, San Francisco, Los Angeles, Seattle, Montreal, Toronto, Vancouver, Mexico City, Havana, Kingston, Ottawa etc.
Climate	: Extending to within 10° of latitude of both the equator and the North Pole, North America has every climatic zone, from tropical rain forest and Savanna on the lowlands of

Central America to areas of permanent ice cap, besides sub-arctic and Tundra climates and arid as well as semi-arid zones.

Facts about South America

Latitude	:	12°N and 55°N
Longitude	:	35°W and 81°W
Area	:	17,820,770 sq. km (approx 12% of the world).
Population	:	386 million (est. 2013)
Ocean and Seas	:	Atlantic Ocean, Pacific Ocean, Caribbean Sea.
Highest and Lowest Points	:	Aconcagua (6,960 m.) and Valdes Penin (-39.9 m.) respectively.
Straits	:	Straits of Magellan
Lakes	:	Lake Maracaibo, Lake Titicaca
Islands	:	Galapagos, Falkland, Tierra del Fuego
Mountains	:	Andes
Plateaus	:	Plateau of Bolivia, Plateau of Equador.
Deserts	:	Atacama, Pantagonia
Rivers	:	Amazon, Orinoco, paraguay, Parana, Uruguay
Important cities	:	Buenos Aires, Rio de Janeiro, Montivideo, Quito, Santiago, La Paz, Lima, Bogota, Valparaiso, Sao Paulo, Belem, Caracas, Manaus.

Facts about Europe

Latitude	:	35°N and 73°N
Longitude	:	25°W and 65°E
Area	:	10,530,750 sq. km (approx.) (7.1%); greatest length north to south 3,860 km; breadth east to west 5,300 km.
Population	:	731,000,000 (est. 2009)
Oceans and Seas	:	Atlantic Ocean, Arctic Ocean, Mediterranean Sea, Caspian Sea, Black Sea, White Sea, North Sea, Norwegian Sea, Baltic Sea, Gulf of Bothnia, Gulf of Finland, Bay of Biscay, Aegean Sea, Adriatic Sea.
Highest and Lowest Points	:	Mt. Elbrus (5,642 m.) and Caspian Sea (–28.0 m.) respectively.
Straits	:	Straits of Gibraltar.
Lakes	:	Lake Ladoga, Onega, Peipus, Vanern, Vaitern.
Islands	:	British Isles, Iceland, Sardinia, Sicily, Crete.

Mountains	:	Alps, Pyrenes, Appenines, Dinaric Alps, Carpathians, Transylvanian Mts., Balkans, Caucasus, Urals.
Plateaus	:	Plateau of Bohemia, Plateau of Spain, Central Massif.
Rivers	:	Volga, Danube, Rhine, Po, Dnieper, Don, Vistula, Elbe, Oder, Seine, Loire, Garrone, Douro, Tagus. Ural.
Important Cities	:	London, Paris, Madrid, Antwerp, Amsterdam, Bonn, Copenhagen, Oslo, Stockholm, Moscow, Frankfurt, Berlin, Warsaw, Venice, Athens, Budapest, Belgrade, Munich, Rome, Prague, Vienna etc.

Facts about Australia

Australia is an island continent and a British Dominion.

Latitude	:	12°S and 38°S
Longitude	:	114°E and 154°E
Area	:	7,830,682 sq. km (5.3%).
Population	:	32 million (est. 2009)
Oceans	:	Pacific Ocean, Indian Ocean.
Seas	:	Tasman Sea, Timor Sea, Arafura Sea, Gulf of Carpentaria, Coral Sea, Great Australian Bight.
Highest Point	:	Puncak Jaya (4884 m) in island of New Guinea [Kosciuszko (2,228 m.) in Australian main land], Mt. Wilhelm (4509 m.) in Papua New Guinea.
Lowest Point	:	lake Eyre (–15.8 m.)
Straits	:	Bass Strait
Lakes	:	Lake Eyre
Islands	:	Tasmania
Mountains	:	Great Dividing Range
Plateaus	:	Western Plateau.
Deserts	:	Gibson Desert, Great Sandy Desert, Great Victoria Desert, Simpson Desert.
Important cities	:	Sydney, Melbourne, Adelaide, Perth, Darwin, Canberra, Brisbane, Hobart.

Oceania

Australia with New Zealand, Tasmania, New Guinea and the Pacific Islands (Micronesian, Melanesian and Polynesian Islands) is called Australasia by some geographers while some others call it "Oceania", which includes proximate islands (Caribbean countries etc.).

Oceans on The Earth

⇨ There are four oceans. In order of their size, they are : Pacific Ocean, Atlantic Ocean, Indian Ocean and Arctic Ocean.

Pacific Ocean

⇨ The explorer *Ferdinand Magellan*, who circumnavigated the Earth, named the ocean "Pacific" meaning calm or peaceful.

⇨ The Pacific Ocean (Area : 166,240,000 sq. km.) is the *largest* ocean of the world.

⇨ It is the *deepest ocean* with an average depth of 4,200 m.

⇨ The *Mariana Trench* is the world's deepest trench with a depth of 11,033 metres (36,201 feet).

⇨ Most of the islands of this ocean are of *volcanic* or *coral origin*.

Atlantic Ocean

⇨ The Atlantic Ocean (Area: 86,560,000 sq. km.) is the *second largest ocean* in the world.

⇨ Its name is derived from Atlas, a Titan (giant) in Greek mythology.

⇨ The Atlantic Ocean has the *longest coastline*.

⇨ The Atlantic Ocean is the *busiest ocean for trade and commerce* since its shipping routes connect the two most industrialized regions, namely Western Europe and N.E. United States of America.

⇨ The Atlantic Ocean was formed millions of years ago when a rift opened up in the Gondwanaland and the continents of South America and Africa separated. The separation continues even today and the Atlantic Ocean is *still widening*.

⇨ The continental islands of *New foundland and British Isles* are the major ones.

⇨ Volcanic islands are fewer and they include those of *Cuba, Jamaica* and *Puerto Rico*. Iceland is the largest island of volcanic origin.

Indian Ocean

⇨ The Indian Ocean (Area : 73,430,000 sq. km.) is the only ocean named after a country.

⇨ The Indian Ocean is *deeper than the Atlantic Ocean.*

⇨ It contains numerous continental islands, Madagascar and Sri Lanka are being the largest ones.

⇨ Some of the islands of volcanic origin are those of *Mauritius, Andaman* and *Nicobar, Seychelles, Maldives* and *Lakshadweep* are of coral origin.

South Indian Ocean
⇨ **Warm currents** : 1. South Equatorial 2. Mozambique 3. Madagascar 4. Agulhas.
⇨ **Cool Currents :** 1. Antarctic drift 2. West Australian currents.

Arctic Ocean
⇨ The Arctic Ocean (Area : 13,230,000 sq. km.) is the *smallest* of all oceans.
⇨ It lies within the Arctic Circle, hence the name Arctic Ocean.
⇨ The *North Pole* lies in the middle of the Arctic Ocean.
⇨ Most of the parts of Arctic Ocean *remains frozen* with thick ice for most of the days every year.
⇨ It is the *shallowest* of all oceans, with an average depth of 1,500 m.
⇨ It has the least salinity of all the oceans. It has a salinity of 20 unit thousand.

Ocean Currents
⇨ The flow of a large amount of water in a definite direction with a great intensity is known as Ocean Current.
⇨ Ocean Currents are of two types-Hot and Cold.

Hot Currents
⇨ The currents flowing from tropical zones of lower latitudes to higher temperate and sub polar zones are-known as hot water currents.

Cold Currents
⇨ The currents flowing from higher latitudes to lower latitudes are known as cold water currents.
⇨ The only exception to the conduction of ocean currents is found in Indian Ocean. The flow of currents changes here with a change in direction of the *Monsoon Winds*. The hot currents flow towards cooler oceans and the cold currents flow towards the warmer oceans.

4. Biosphere
⇨ The part of the Earth where life exists is called the *Biosphere* ('bios' means 'life').
⇨ The Earth is the only planet of the solar system that supports life. Life is possible because of its unique lithosphere, hydrosphere and atmosphere.

5. Lithosphere
⇨ The uppermost layer of the Earth's crust which is capable of supporting life is called *Lithosphere*.
⇨ The Lithosphere (or land) covers two-sevenths or 29.22% (14,90,41,182 sq. km.) of the total surface area of the earth.

6. Hydrosphere

➩ Hydrosphere (or sea) covers five-sevenths or more accurately 70.78% (36,10,59,226 sq. km) of the total surface area of the earth.
➩ Water is freely available in the gaseous, liquid and solid state.
➩ It is necessary for carrying out chemical reactions within the bodies of the living organisms.
➩ Water also dissolves and transports nutrients from the soil to the plants.
➩ It is used by plants for making food.

7. The Earth

The earth or the 'blue planet' is the only planet that is known to be inhabitable. It is called the blue planet because it is composed of more than 71 percent of water. Land covers only 29 percent of the total area. The earth is spherical in shape. Its total surface area is around 5, 09,700,000 sq.km. The estimated weight of the planet is 5.94 10 power 19 metric tonnes.

The earth is composed of various elements. The major ones are listed below:

Elements	Percentage	Elements	Percentage
Oxygen	46.5%	Calcium	3.63%
Silicon	27.72%	Sodium	2.85%
Aluminium	8.13%	Potassium	2.62%
Iron	5.01%	Magnesium	2.09%

The earth is divided into the following layers:

Crust	The outermost layer of the earth is composed of crystalline rocks. It consists of about 0.374% of the earth's mass and has a depth of around 0.31 miles (0-50 kilometres).
Mantle	It lies under the crust and is composed of silicon, oxygen, magnesium, iron, aluminium and calcium. It has a thickness of 2900 km.
Core	This is an iron-nickel core that is about 2,100 miles in radius. It has two parts.
	➩ The inner core is solid and has a temperature going up to 13,000°F (7,200°C = 7,500 K). It has a radius of about 1,228 km.
	➩ The outer core is in a liquid state and is about 2,260 km thick.

Important Areas and Terms of the Earth

Equator	It is the imaginary line which lies at an equal distance from both the north and south poles- 0 to 10 degrees north and 0 to 10 degrees south.
Tropic of Cancer	It lies parallel to the equator at 23.5 degrees north.
Tropic of Cancer	This too lies parallel to the equator, but at 23.5 degrees south.
Subtropical	It is the area between 23.5 degrees south and 40 degrees south and 23.5 degrees north and 40 degrees north.
Antarctic Circle	It is the parallel of 66.5 degrees south.
Arctic Circle	It is the parallel of 66.5 degrees north.
Latitude	This is the imaginary line which lies parallel to the equator. It ranges from 0 degree that is from the equator to the poles that is 90 degrees north/south.
Parallel	This is a line that joins all points of the same latitude. One degree latitude would be 111 km.
Longitude	It is estimated from the Prime Meridian, in a west to east direction, from 0 to 180 degrees meridian.
Meridian	It is a line that joins all points on the same longitude. They are not parallel to one another, except at the equator.
Greenwich Meridian Time (GMT)	It is the mean solar time or the standard time in London, U.K. It was the global time standard till 1972 when the Coordinated Universal Time (UTC) replaced it.
Local Time	It is the time which is determined by the position of the sun over a particular place. The local time of different places varies, starting from GMT going at the rate of four minutes for each longitude.
Standard time	It is the established time of a country. This is determined by the positioning of a central meridian upon which the most important city would be located. The Central Meridian is selected such that it is divisible by 7.5 degrees, so that the standard time stands dissimilar to the GMT in multiples of half an hour.

International Date Line (IDL)	It is the imaginary line on the surface of the earth which follows the 180 degree meridian of longitude. It was decided in the International Conference (1884) that there would be a single universal day which would start at midnight at Greenwich, London. Travellers who cross the IDL from a west to east direction repeat a day, while those who cross from east to west lose a day.
Equinox	These are those dates when day and night are equal in their duration. There is the Vernal Equinox on March 21 and the Autumnal Equinox on September 23.
Solstice	These are those dates when the difference between day and night is the largest. The Summer Solstice is on June 21 and the Winter Solstice is on **December 22.**

Movements of the Earth

Rotation	The earth's movement in a west-east direction on its designated imaginary axis is called *rotation*. It takes approximately 24 hours for the earth to complete one rotation. This movement is responsible for days and nights.
	In the southern hemisphere, December 22 is the longest day and June 21 is the shortest. In the Northern Hemisphere, June 21 is the longest day while, December 21 is the shortest. Days and nights are equal at the equator all throughout the year.
Revolution	This is the time taken by the earth to move around the sun. One revolution takes 365 days, 6 hours, 9 minutes and 9.54 seconds. Revolutions are responsible for season changes.

8. Atmosphere

The earth's atmosphere is a colourless, odourless, tasteless mixture of gases along with moisture and fine dust. It forms a layer over the planet. It has a height of about 700 km.

The atmosphere acts as a protective shield against harmful UV radiations from the sun. It also prevents heat from escaping at night.

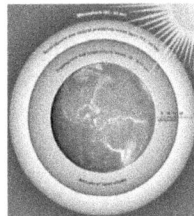

Composition of gases in the atmosphere:

Nitrogen	78.09%	Argon	0.93%
Oxygen	20.95%	Carbondioxide	0.03%
Neon	0.0018%	Helium	0.0005%
Ozone	0.0006%	Hydrogen	0.00006%

9. Layers of the Atmosphere

There are five distinct layers of the atmosphere — (a) Troposphere (b) Stratosphere (c) Mesosphere (d) Thermosphere and (e) Exosphere.

Troposphere

⇨ This is the first layer of the atmosphere. It extends to a height of *18 km at the equator* and *8 km at the poles*.

⇨ In this layer temperature decreases with height. This is due to the fact that the density of air decreases with height and so the heat absorbed is less. It contains more than 90% of gases in the atmosphere.

⇨ Since most of the water vapour form clouds in this layer, all weather changes occur in the troposphere (*"tropo"* means 'change').

⇨ The height at which the *temperature stops decreasing* is called *tropopause*. Here the temperature may be as low as *–58°C*.

Stratosphere

⇨ This is the *second layer* of the atmosphere. It extends from the *tropopause* to *about 50 km*.

⇨ Temperature increases due to the absorption of the *ultraviolet radiation* of the Sun by *ozone* present in this layer. The temperature slowly increases to *4°C*.

⇨ This layer is free from clouds and associated weather phenomena.

⇨ Hence, it provides ideal flying conditions for large jet planes.

⇨ At about 50 km the *temperature begins to fall again*. This marks the end of the stratosphere. The end of the stratosphere is called the *stratopause*.

Mesosphere

⇨ Above the stratosphere lies the mesosphere.

⇨ The mesosphere extends to a height of *80 km*.

⇨ Here the temperature decreases again, falling as low as *–90°C*.

⇨ The end of this layer is known as the *mesopause*.

Thermosphere

⇨ The thermosphere lies above the mesosphere.

⇨ This layer extends to a height of about *640 km*.

⇨ In this layer temperature rises dramatically, reaching upto *1480°C*.

⇨ This increase in temperature is due to the fact that the gas molecules in this layer absorb the *X-rays* and *ultraviolet radiation* of the Sun.

⇨ This results in the break up of the gas molecules into *positively* and *negatively charged particles or ions*. Thus, this layer is also known as the *ionosphere*.
⇨ The electrically charged gas molecules of the thermosphere reflect radio waves from the Earth back into space. Thus, this layer also helps in long distance communications.
⇨ The thermosphere also protects us from meteors and obsolete satellites, because its high temperature burns up nearly all the debris coming towards the Earth.

Exosphere
⇨ This layer lies above the thermosphere.
⇨ The exosphere extends beyond the thermosphere upto *960 km*.
⇨ It gradually merges with interplanetary space.
⇨ The temperatures in this layer range from about *300°C* to *1650°C*.
⇨ This layer contains only traces of gases like oxygen, nitrogen, argon and helium because the lack of gravity allows the gas molecules to escape easily into space.

10. Winds

Trade Winds	A steady wind blowing towards the equator from the north-east in the northern hemisphere and the south-east in the southern hemisphere. There are two belts of *trade winds* which encircle the earth. They blow from the tropical high-pressure belts to the low-pressure zone at the equator. These are the most regular of all the planetary winds. When passing over oceans, they gather moisture and shower heavy rain over the east coast of the continents.
Westerlies	These winds travel from the *sub-tropical high pressure areas* to the *sub-polar low pressure areas*. They are not as consistent or constant as the trade winds.
Easterlies	These winds travel from the polar high pressure belts to the temperate low pressure belts. They are variable cold and dry winds.
Local Winds	These are of the following types:
	Mistral — Very cold winds that blow down from the Alps over France.
	Sirocca — Moist and hot wind that blows from the Sahara Desert to the Mediterranean Sea.
	Levanter — Cold wind present in Spain.
	Santa Ana — Hot wind present in South California.
	Punas — Dry and cold wind that blows towards western Andes.

Foehn	Hot and dry winds present in the Alps.
Bora	Dry and cold wind that flows in an outward direction from *Hungary to northern Italy.*
Khamsin	Dry and hot wind present in Egypt.
Brick Fielder	Hot wind present in Australia
Norwester	Hot wind present in New Zealand.

11. Cyclones and Anticyclones

A *cyclone* is a type of storm wherein there is low pressure centre which is surrounded by increasing high pressure conditions on the outside. The wind blows in a circular manner. It blows in a clockwise direction in the southern hemisphere and in an anti-clockwise direction in the northern hemisphere.

Cyclones are known by different names in different places:

Countries	Cyclones
West Indies	*Hurricane*
China	*Typhoon*
North-West Australia	*Willy or Willies*
Coastal USA	*Tornado*

Anticyclones are opposite to the cyclones. There is high atmospheric pressure at the centre around which air circulates slowly. These are associated with a calm weather.

12. Climate

Tropical Rainforest	Also known as *Equatorial Forest*, this type of climate is found in 5 degrees to 10 degrees north and to the south of the equator. The average monthly temperature in this climate is 24-27 degrees celsius and the average rainfall is 250 cm. Green and dense forests are found abundantly. Such a climate is prevalent in the Amazon Basin, the Congo Basin and Indonesia.
Monsoon	The rainfall in this climate is seasonal, and the average downpour is 200 cm. The average temperature is 30 degrees celsius. Deciduous forests are found in this climate.
Tropical Savannah	Temperatures in this climate are always high. The average rainfall is 150 cm and seasonal. Trees that are fire-resistant and having longer roots are generally found. Grasslands, scattered trees and bushes are also found.

Tropical-Subtropical Hot Desert	This climatic region experiences dry summer and humid winters, with an average summer temperature of 25 degrees celsius and winter temperature ranging from 4 degrees to 10 degrees celsius. Such a climate is found in the trade wind belt in the western belt of continents. Exotic fruits such as grapes and citrus fruits, and olives are found in this region.
Taiga	Coniferous forests are found in this region. The word, 'Taiga' means *coniferous or snow forests*. Winters are very cold with temperatures going below 0 degree celsius. The average summer temperature is 10 degrees celsius and the average rainfall is 50 centimetres.
Tundra	This is a very *cold climate type*, where the subsoil is always frozen. Rainfall is less than 30 cm. This kind of climate is found in the Arctic region of Europe, North America and Asia. Mosses and lichens are common vegetations found here.

13. Clouds

Clouds are masses of condensed water vapour in the atmosphere. They lie high above the ground. They are formed when the air cools into dew and then the vapour condenses into water droplets.

Clouds are of the following types:

High Level Clouds	They are situated at a height above 20,000 feet (6,000 metres) and because of cold temperatures, they are composed of ice crystals. High-level clouds are thin and white in appearance.
Mid-Level Clouds	These appear between 6,500 to 20,000 feet (2,000 to 6,000 metres). They are composed of water droplets because of low altitudes. They can also be composed of ice crystals when temperatures are low.
Low-Level Clouds	These are composed of water droplets because they lie below 6,500 feet (2,000 metres).
Vertically Developed Clouds	These are formed either through thermal convection or frontal lifting. These clouds can grow to heights of about 39,000 feet (12,000 metres).

14. Latitude and Longitude

Any location on Earth is described by two numbers—its *latitude* and its *longitude*.

Latitude

On a globe of the Earth, lines of latitude are circles of different size. The longest is the equator, whose latitude is zero, while at the poles-at latitudes 90° north and 90° south (or -90°) the circles shrink to a point.

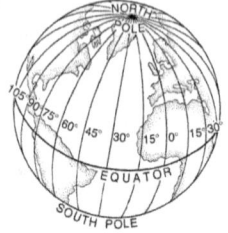

Longitude

On the globe, lines of constant longitude ('meridians') extend from pole to pole.

Every meridian must cross the equator. Since the equator is a circle, we can divide it like any circle — into 360 degrees, and the longitude of a point is then the marked value of that division where its meridian meets the equator.

For historical reasons, the longitude (meridian) passing the old Royal Astronomical Observatory in *Greenwich, England*, is the one chosen as *zero longitude*. Located at the eastern edge of London, the British capital, the observatory is now a public museum and a brass band stretching across its yard marks the *"prime meridian."*

> A line of longitude is also called a *meridian*, derived from the Latin, from meri, a variation of *"medius"* which denotes *"middle"*, and diem, meaning *"day."* The word once meant "noon", and times of the day before noon were known as *"ante meridian"*, while times after it were *"post meridian."* Today's abbreviations a.m. and p.m. come from these terms, and the Sun at noon was said to be *"passing meridian"*. All points on the same line of longitude experienced noon (and any other hour) at the same time and were therefore said to be on the same *"meridian line"*.

Local Time (LT) and Time Zones

Two important concepts, related to latitude and (especially) longitude are *Local time (LT)* and *Universal time (UT)*

Longitudes are measured from zero to 180° east and 180° west (or −180°), and both 180 degree longitudes share the same line, in the middle of the *Pacific Ocean*.

As the Earth rotates around its axis, at any moment one line of longitude-"the noon meridian"—faces the Sun, and at that moment, it will be noon everywhere on it. After 24 hours the Earth has undergone a full rotation with respect to the Sun, and the same meridian again faces noon. Thus each hour the Earth rotates by 360/24 = 15 degrees.

The Date Line and Universal Time (UT)

Longitude determines only the hour of the day—not the date, which is determined separately. The international date line has been established most of it following the 180th meridian—where by common agreement, whenever we cross it the date advances one day (going west) or goes back one day (going east).

That line passes the *Bering Strait* between Alaska and Siberia, which thus have different dates, but for most of its course it runs in mid-ocean and does not inconvenience any local time keeping.

Astronomers, astronauts and people dealing with satellite data may need a time schedule which is the same everywhere, not tied to a locality or time zone. The *Greenwich mean time*, the astronomical time at Greenwich (averaged over the year) is generally used here. It is sometimes called Universal Time (UT).

15. Heat Zones of The Earth

Torrid Zone

▷ This is also referred to as Tropical zone. The Tropics is a region on the Earth surrounding Eqauator by the Tropic of Cancer in. the northern hemisphere at $23°26'16''$ N (approx) and the Tropic of Capricorn in the sourthern hemisphere at $23°26'16''$ S (approx). The Tropics include all the areas on the Earth where the sun reaches a point directly overhed at least once in a year.

▷ This area receives *maximum heat* and is called the *Torrid (hot) Zone.*

Frigid Zone

▷ Near the polar regions, the rays of the Sun are very slanting and so it is *very cold.*

▷ The region/area between the Arctic Circle and the North Pole in the Northern Hemisphere is called the *Frigid Zone.*

▷ There are similar regions in the Southern Hemisphere between the Antarctic Circle and the South Pole, also called the Frigid Zone (frigid means cold).

Rotation of the Earth

▷ The Earth spins (rotates), west to east on its axis once in 24 hours approximately.

▷ The Earth's axis is not vertical. It makes an angle of $23°30'$ with the vertical or $66°30'$ with the plane of the Earth's orbit.

▷ The Earth's axis always remains pointed in the same direction (towards the Pole Star) as the Earth moves around the Sun. The tilt of the Earth's axis is known as the inclination of the Earth's axis.

16. Effect of the Tilted Axis on Day and Night

▷ Rotation of the Earth on its tilted axis causes days and nights to be of different length in different parts of the Earth.

⇨ Since the Earth's axis is tilted in the same direction, the orientation of the Earth's axis to the Sun's rays is constantly changing as the Earth moves around the Sun. This results in a continuous change in the length of days and nights throughout the year.

Perihelion
⇨ The position of the earth or any other planet in its orbit when it is at its nearest point to the sun.
⇨ The earth reaches its perihelion about 3rd January at a distance of about 147 million kilometer near one extremity of the major axis of the earth's elliptical orbit, the axis being called Apsides line.

Aphelion
⇨ The position of the earth or any other planet in its orbit when it is at its distant point from the sun.
⇨ The earth reaches its aphelion on 4th July when the earth is at a distance of 152 million kilometer near the other extremity of the major axis.

Solstice
⇨ Solstice is one of the two dates in the year on which the sun reaches greatest altitude north or south of the equator and is directly overhead along one of the lines of the tropics.

Summer Solstice
⇨ On June 21, the earth is so located in its orbit that the sun is overhead on the Tropic of Cancer (23½°N).
⇨ On this date the northern hemisphere is tipped towards the sun having the *longest day*, while the southern hemisphere is tipped away from the sun having the shortest day.

Winter Solstice
⇨ On December 22, the earth is in an equivalent position on the opposite points in its orbit, so the southern hemisphere is tipped towards the sun and the northern hemisphere away from it.
⇨ The sun is overhead on the Tropic of Capricorn (23½°S), resulting in the *shortest day* in the northern hemisphere.

Equinoxes
⇨ Two days in a year when day and night are equal throughout the world are equinoxes.
⇨ Falling midway between the dates of solstices, on these dates, the earth's axis lies at 90° to the line joining the centres of the earth and the sun and neither the northern nor the southern hemisphere is inclined towards the sun.
⇨ The *'vernal equinox'* occurs on *March 21* and it is also called the *spring equinox* in the northern hemisphere.
⇨ The 'autumnal equinox' occurs on September 23.

Midnight Sun

- ⇨ This phenomenon is observed in the Arctic and Antarctic zones around mid-summer, when the sun does not sink below the horizon throughout 24 hours of the day and therefore, may be seen at midnight.
- ⇨ This is the direct consequence of the inclination of the axis of the earth to the plane of the orbit.
- ⇨ Norway is the *place of midnight sun* where the sun is continuously visible between May and July.
- ⇨ In the southern hemisphere, the phenomenon is seen in the Antarctica continent.

Eclipses

- ⇨ An Eclipse occurs when the sun, moon and earth are in a straight line.
- ⇨ A *'solar eclispe'* occurs between sunrise and sunset on new moon when the moon passes directly in front of the sun so that its shadow lies on the earth. In other words, the moon lies between the sun and the earth.
- ⇨ The 'lunar eclipse'takes place when the earth comes in between the sun and the moon so that the shadow of the earth is cast on the moon.
- ⇨ A lunar eclipse takes place on a full moon.
- ⇨ Generally a total of seven eclipses, including solar and lunar eclipses, take place every year.

16. Weather and Climate

- ⇨ *Weather* is the description of the atmospheric conditions of a particular place at a particular time for a short period of time.
- ⇨ *Climate* is the composite or integrated picture of the weather conditions over a long period of time.
- ⇨ *Climatic data* is based on calculated averages of data recorded over a period of 35 years. The classical period is 30 years, as defined by WMO.

Atmospheric Pressure

- ⇨ Atmospheric pressure is the pressure at any point on the surface of the Earth due to the weight of the column of air above that point.

Measurement and Units of Atmospheric Pressure

- ⇨ The *mercury barometer* is the standard instrument for measuring atmospheric pressure.
- ⇨ Pressure is expressed in *centimeters* or *inches of mercury,* a true measure of the height of the mercury column.

Pressure Measuring Instruments

1. Mercurial Barometer (or Fortin's Barometer)
2. Aneroid Barometer
3. Altimeter or Altitude Barometer
4. Barograph (automatic recording Aneroid Barometer)
5. Microbarometer
6. Microbarovariograph

- *Standard sea level pressure is 76 cm or 29.92 inches on this scale.*
- Another pressure unit used by meteorologists in drawing weather charts is *millibars (mb.)*
- One bar is divided into 1000 millibars.
- Millibars are now known as *hectopascals*.

17. Internal Structure of The Earth

The Earth's Crust

- The outermost solid cover or shell of the earth is known as the earth's *crust*.
- The thickness of the crust is about 30 km.
- It is thicker in the region of the continents and thinner in the region of the ocean floors.
- The density of the rocks in the earth's crust ranges from 2.7 to 3 g/c.c (grams per cubic centimeter).
- The upper part of the crust consists of silica and aluminium in greater proportions. That is why, it is called '*Sial*'.
- Whereas the lower part of the crust is called '*Sima*' because the proportion of silica and magnesium is higher in this part.

Mantle

- This layer lies below the crust.
- Its thickness is about 2900 km and the density of substances in the mantle ranges from 3.0 to 4.7.

Core

- The earth's *core* lies below the mantle. Its thickness may be about 3471 km.
- Its *radius* is 6371 km., according to IUGG.
- It is divided into two parts, the outer core and the inner core. The outer core is probably in a liquid state and the inner core in a solid state.
- The core mainly consists of iron with some amount of nickel and sulphur (NIFE).
- After the mantle, the earth's density goes on increasing rapidly towards its centre and finally is more than 13.
- The temperature of the central part of the earth may be about 5000°C.
- The study of the earth's interior helps us to understand the original rocks in the earth's crust and their later transformation.

18. Rocks

- The *solid parts of the earth's crust are called rocks*. Most of the rocks are made up of two or more minerals.
- In the same type of rocks, the proportions of minerals may be different in different areas.
- Rocks may not always necessarily be hard.
- Minerals are obtained from rocks.

➪ Rocks are classified in three main types depending on the process of their formation: (a) Igneous, (b) Sedimentary, (c) Metamorphic.

Igneous rocks

➪ Hot *lava* pours out at the time of volcanic eruptions and cools down later on, forming rocks.

➪ The molten materials known as *magma*, sometimes cool down beneath the earth's crust, again forming rocks.

➪ Both these types of rocks are known as *Igneous rocks*.

➪ When the earth's surface first became solid after it cooled down from its hot liquid state, the original rocks of the earth's crust were formed. They are the Primary Igneous rocks, which are usually not found today.

➪ Igneous rocks are generally *harder and granular*.

➪ There are *no layers* in Igneous rocks.

➪ Fossils are not found in Igneous rocks.

➪ The formation of Igneous rocks takes place beneath and above the surface of the earth.

➪ Rocks formed by the cooling of molten matter beneath the earth's surface are called *intrusive igneous rocks*. 'Granite' and 'Gabbro' are the main examples of these rocks.

➪ The intrusive rocks are thus crystalline rocks.

➪ Sometimes, the molten matter oozes out through cracks in the earth's crust and spreads on the surface, forming *extrusive igneous rocks*.

➪ Gabbro, Obsidian, Basalt etc. are examples of extrusive igneous rocks.

➪ A very large area of the *Deccan Plateau* consists of basalt rocks.

➪ These rocks contain silica from 40 to 80%, others are feldspar, magnesium and iron etc.

Igneous rocks	Metamorphic rocks
Granite	Gneiss
Gabbro	Sarpentine

➪ Other examples of lgneous rocks are – Granite, Pumic stone, Basalt and Gabbro.

Sedimentary rocks

➪ They are formed by the deposition, sedimentation and lethification of sediments over a long period of time.

➪ As layers over layers get deposited, over a period of time, unified sedimentary rocks are formed on account of the tremendous pressure exerted by the layers above.

➪ Sometimes the remains of plants, dead animals etc. are found in the deposited material. Such fossil containing sedimentary rocks are useful for studying life on earth.

Sedimentary rocks	Metamorphic rocks
Limestone	Marble
Sandstone	Quartzite
Shale/clay	State, Phyllite, Schist
Coal	Diamond

- Sandstone, limestone, shale are some examples of sedimentary rocks.
- *Limestone* is white as well as black.
- *Sandstone* is dull white, pink, bright red or sometimes black.

Metmaorphic rocks
- The nature of igneous and sedimentary rocks changes due to the effects of tremendous heat or pressure, and new, transformed rocks, called *metamorphic rocks*, are formed.
- Minerals in the rocks get restructured on account of heat and pressure. This brings about a change in the original formation of the rocks.

Some examples of metamorphic rocks formed from igneous and sedimentary rocks.

Type of rock	Original rock	Metamorphic rock
Igneous	granite	gneiss
Igneous	basalt	homblend
Sedimentary	limestone	marble
Sedimentary	coal	graphite coal
Sedimentary	sandstone	quartzite
Sedimentary	shale/clay	slate, mica schist

19. Earthquakes and Volcanoes

Earth Quakes
- The sudden tremors or shaking of the earth's crust is called an *earthquake*. When a part of the earth's surface moves backward and forward or up and down, the earth's surface 'quakes', and these are called the 'earthquake'.
- The earth's crust is made up of different parts of various sizes. They are called plates.
- Most of the earthquakes in the world are caused by the movements of the plates.
- *'Seismology'* the special branch of Geology, It deals with the study of earthquake.
- *'Richter scale'* and *'Mercalli scale'* are the instruments to measure/record the *magnitude* and the *intensity* of an earthquake respectively.

Seismic Waves
- The place where the seismic waves originate beneath the earth's surface is called the *focus of the earthquake*.
- The *epicenter* is that point on the ground surface which is closest to the focus.
- Seismic waves are recorded on the *seismograph*. Seismic waves are mainly of three types-(i) Primary waves (ii) Secondary waves and (iii) Surface or Long waves.

The earthquake zones in India

⇨ The Indian plate is moving from south to north. That is why there are earthquakes in the Himalayan region.

⇨ Earthquakes occur in Assam, Arunachal Pradesh, Nagaland, Tripura, Manipur, Mizoram, Andaman and Nicobar Islands, Jammu and Kashmir, the north-western region of Uttar Pradesh, the northern region of Bihar etc.

⇨ During the last few years, there have been several earthquakes of varying mtensities in Maharashtra and Gujarat.

Volcanic Activity

⇨ Magma or molten rock is formed beneath the ground surface due to various reasons.

⇨ This molten rock ruptures the ground and pours out. Sometimes, it cools down beneath the ground surface instead of pouring out.

⇨ All these activities are called *volcanic activities*.

⇨ Volcanic activities have been taking place since times immemorial.

⇨ There are three types of Volcanoes :
   (i) Active Volcanoes (ii) Dormant Volcanoes (iii) Extinct Volcanoes.

Volcanic eruptions

⇨ The pouring out of the magma or molten rock through ground surface is called a *volcanic eruption*.

⇨ At the time of eruption, the magma, steam, fragments of rock, dust and gaseous substances are ejected with great force from under the ground surface through a pipe like passage.

⇨ The opening of this pipe on the earth's surface is known as the vent which forms a *crater*.

⇨ The *lava* which is thrown into the sky during an eruption, falls to the ground in the form of solid fragments. Dark clouds gather in the sky and it begins to rain heavily.

⇨ The volcanic ash and dust mixes with the rainwater giving rise to hot mud flows.

Types of Volcanic Eruptions

⇨ Volcanic eruptions are classified into two types depending on the manner of ejection of the magma :
   (i) Central eruption, (ii) Fissure eruption.

Central eruption

⇨ This type of eruption is sometimes very explosive, because lava, steam, gas, dust, smoke, stone fragments are ejected from a narrow pipe from under the ground with greater intensity. This type of eruption gives rise to conical or dome-shaped hills.

Some examples of volcanic mountains formed due to central eruption are *Mt. Kilimanjaro* in Africa, the *Fujiyama* in Japan and the *Vesuvius* and *Mount Etna* in Italy.

⇨ It is basically poured acidic lava.

Fissure eruption

⇨ A very long fissure (cracks) develops in the ground surface and so, the molten rock, rock fragments, steam and gases within, pour out slowly.

⇨ These eruptions take place at a very slow speed. Since this lava is more fluid, it spreads over longer distances.

⇨ The lava cools down on the ground over a period of time, increasing the thickness of the surface in that area. *Basalt* plateaus are formed due to these eruptions.

⇨ Basalt plateaus are also found in Brazil in South America and Saudi Arabia in West Asia and Deccan plateau in India.

⇨ In Maharashtra, the fertile black regur soil has been formed from basalt rocks. It is also called *black cotton soil.*

20. Various Landforms

Mainly there are three types of landforms – Mountains, Plateaus, Plains.

Mountains

The height of mountains are over 600 m and have conical peaks. On the basis of origin there are four types of mountains: Block Mountains, Residual Mountains, Accumulated Mountains and Fold Mountains.

Block Mountains

⇨ The middle part of such mountains is lower and the parts on both the sides are higher.The middle lower portion is called as *Rift valley.* The longest rift valley is the valley of the Jordan river.

⇨ Black Forest (Germany), Vindhyachal and Satpura (India), Salt Range (Pakistan) are some examples of block mountains.

Residual Mountains

⇨ Such mountains are formed as a result of weathering. Examples Aravalli, Nilgiri, Parasnath, Hills of Rajmahal (India), Siera (Spain).

Accumulated Mountains

⇨ These are formed due to accumulation of sand, soil, rocks, lava etc. on the Earth's Crust., e.g. Sand Dunes.

Fold Mountains

⇨ These are formed because of the folds in the rocks due to internal motions of the earth. These are wavelike mountains which have numerous peaks and lows, e.g. Himalayas, Ural, Alps, Rockies, Andes etc.

Plateaus

⇨ Plateaus are extensive upland areas characterised by flat and rough top surface and steep walls which rise above the neighbouring ground surface at least for 300 m.

⇨ Generally the height of plateau ranges from 300 to 500 feet.

Intermountainous Plateaus : Plateaus formed between mountain, Example-Tibetan Plateau.

Mountainstep Plateaus : The flat region between a plain and the base of a mountain.

Continental Plateaus : These are formed when the Lacolith inside the Earth comes to the surface due to weathering. e.g. the Southern Plateau.

Bank Plateaus : These are the plateaus on the banks of the oceans.

Plateaus having more than average height	
Tibetan Plateau	16000 ft
Bolivian Plateau	11800 ft
Columbian Plateau	7800 ft

Domelike Plateaus: These are formed due to the movement of man and animals on the surface. e.g. Ramgarh Plateau.

Plains

Plains can be defined as flat areas with low height (below 500ft.)

Weathered Plains : The plains formed due to weathering by rivers, glaciers, winds etc.

Loess Plains : These are formed by the soil and sands brought by winds.

Karst Plains : Plains formed due to the weathering of limestone.

Erosional Plains : Plains near the river banks formed by river erosion.

Glacial Plains : Marshy plains formed due to the deposition of ice.

Desert Plains : These are formed as a result of the flow of rivers.

Deposition Plains : Large plains are formed due to the silt brought by the rivers. Such plains are plains of Ganga, Sutlej, Mississipi, Hwang Ho.

Forests

They are of the following types :

(a) **Tropical Evergreen Rain Forests:** Such forests are found in the equatorial and the tropical regions with more than 200 ems annual rainfall. The leaves of trees in such forests are very wide. Ex- Red wood, palm etc.

(b) **Tropical Semi Deciduous Forests :** Such forests recieve rainfall less than 150 cms. Saagwan, saal, bamboo etc. are found in such forests.

(c) **Temperate mixed Forests :** Such forests are a mixture of trees and shrubs. Corks, Oak etc. are the major trees of these forests.

(d) **Coniferous Forests or Taiga:** These are evergreen forests. The trees, in these forests, have straight trunk, conical shape with relatively short branches and small needlelike leaves. Example-Pine, Fir etc.

(e) **Tundra Forests:** Such forests are covered with snow. Only Mosses, a few sladges and Lichens grow here in the summers. This type of vegetation is chiefly confined to the northern hemisphere (e.g. in Eurasia, North America and Greenland Coaste).

(f) Mountainous Forests : Vegetation varies according to altitude.

Pastures (or Grasslands)

⇨ They can be divided into two types :

(i) Tropical Pastures and (ii) Temperate Pastures

Tropical Pastures : They have different names in different countries. Savanna in Africa, Campos in Brazil, Lanos in Venezuela and Columbia.

Temperate Pastures : They are known by the following names-Praries in USA and Canada, Pampas in Argentina, Veld in South Africa, Downs in Australia, in Newzealand, Steppes in Eurasia (Ukraine, Russia).

Land forms created by the river system
V-shaped valley

⇨ A river flows with a greater velocity in the mountainous region and big, pointed fragments of rock also flow with a great speed along with the water.

⇨ The river bed is scoured and downcutting starts, ultimately giving rise to a deep valley with steep sides. This valley is called a *v-shaped valley*.

⇨ These valleys are found in mountainous regions.

⇨ A deep and narrow valley with steep sides is called a gorge.

⇨ The gorge of the river *Ulhas in Thane* district in Maharashtra and the gorge of the river Narmada at Bhedaghat near Jabalpur in Madhya Pradesh are well known.

⇨ There are many gorges in the Himalayas.

Waterfall

⇨ If there are both hard (resistant) and soft (less resistant) rocks in the course of the river, the less resistant rock is eroded faster.

⇨ The resistant rock does not erode so easily. That is why, the river falls with a great speed from a cliff-like part of hard rock. This is called a *waterfall*.

⇨ The *Niagara Falls* on the Niagara river is in North America.

Potholes

⇨ In areas where the river bed consists of hard rock, the stones carried along with the river water due to the whirling impact of water.

⇨ That is why holes of various shapes are formed in the rocky river bed. Such holes are called *potholes*.

⇨ Many patholes are observed in the river bed of the Kukadi, Krishna, Godavari etc. in Maharashtra.

Meanders and ox-bow lakes

⇨ Meanders are formed by lateral erosion. As the erosion increases over a period of time, the meanders in the river again starts flowing in a straight line.

⇨ The loop previously formed then separates from the main course of the river. Water accumulates in this separated part.

⇨ As this loop resembles on ox-bow it is called ox-bow lake. It formed due to impounding of water in the abandoned meander loop.

Fan-shaped plains

⇨ In the region near the source of a river the tributaries joining the main river deposit materials carried by them on the banks of the main river.

⇨ This deposition creates fan-like plains. They are called fan-shaped plains or alluvial fans.

Flood plains

⇨ When, during the floods, the river-water overflows its banks and spreads in the surrounding areas, the silt carried by the water gets deposited in those areas. This creates flat plains on both the banks of the river. Plains created by this depositional work done during floods are called *flood plains*.

⇨ The Gangetic Plain is a flood plain.

Natural levees

⇨ When a river is over flooded, its water crosses its banks. At that time, the speed of the water is reduced, and the pebbles and stones carried by the river get deposited near the banks.

⇨ On account of frequent floods, the area where these sediments .are deposited near the bank of the river rises higher than the flood plam

⇨ This high wall is called a *natural levee* or *natural embankment*.

⇨ Such levees are found on the banks of the Mississippi, the Huang-ho etc., Southern bank of river Ganga.

Delta

⇨ Delta was coined by Herodotus (the 'Father of History') after the Greek letter delta (Δ) because of the deltoid shape at the mouth of the Nile.

⇨ A delta is a land form that is formed at the mouth of a river where that river flows into an ocean, sea, estuary, lake, reservoir, flat arid area or another river.

⇨ Deltas are formed from the deposition of the sediment carried by the river as the flow leaves the mouth of the river. Over long periods of lime, this deposition builds the characteristic geographic pattern of a river delta.

Delta-region

⇨ A river meets a sea or a lake. The silt carried by the river is deposited on the bed near its mouth.

⇨ The area near the mouth of the river gets gradually filled up by this deposition and gets raised causing an obstruction for the river to flow in a single channel. It, therefore, splits into two branches and meets the sea.

⇨ Over a period of time, there is deposition also at the mouth of these branches. In this manner, the main course of the river gets split into a network of small channels. These sub-channels are called *distributaries*.

⇨ A triangular region of innumerable such distributaries is formed near the mouth of the river. This region is called the *delta region*.

⇨ There are *delta regions* near the *vent* (opening) of the rivers Godavari, Ganga, Nile, Mississippi etc. Deltas are very fertile.

⇨ The largest delta of the world is 'Sunderbans Delta' (350 km.).

Land forms created by the actions of river

Erosion	Erosion Deposition	Deposition
V-shaped valley	Meanders	Fan-shaped plains
Gorge	Ox-bow	Flood Plains
Potholes	Lakes	Delta
Waterfall		Natural Levees

Glacier

⇨ A mass of ice sliding down the slope from a snow-clad region is called a glacier. On an average a glacier moves 1 to 15 metres a day.

⇨ While a glacier is moving, the friction of the ice at the bottom slows down the movement of the bottom layers.

⇨ There are two main types of glaciers : (i) Continental Glacier, and (ii) Alpine Glacier.

Continental Glacier

⇨ An extensive sheet of ice spreading across a vast region sometimes begins to move due to the pressure of the ice.

⇨ This moving sheet of ice is called a *continental glacier*.

⇨ Such glaciers are seen in Antarctica and Greenland.

Alpine or mountain glacier

⇨ There are snow-field in the mountainous regions of the Himalayas, the

⇨ Alps, the Andes, the Rocky mountains etc.

⇨ The ice accumulating in these areas starts sliding down the slopes.

⇨ This mass of ice sliding down from the mountains is called a *mountain glacier* or an *alpine glacier*.

Iceberg
▷ Blocks of ice break off from the continental glaciers and float away into the sea.
▷ A block of ice floating in the sea is called an *iceberg*. These icebergs are huge in size.
▷ The density of ice being slightly less than that of water, a very little portion of an iceberg is seen above the water and the rest of it is submerged under water.

Land forms Created by Glacier
▷ Various land forms are created on account of the transportation, erosion and depositional work of a glacier. Let us consider the major land forms thus created.

Cirque
▷ When the snow from the mountain peaks slides, it gets deposited in a hollow, if there is one on any side of the peak.
▷ The accumulated snow starts sliding down the slope. This causes friction at the floor and at the sides of the hollow, thus enlarging it further. This is called a *cirque*.
▷ The back wall of a cirque is like a high cliff and the floor is concave and huge in size. The total shape resembles an *armchair*.
▷ When a glacier melts completely, water accumulates in the cirque and forms a lake which is known as *tarn*.

Fiord
▷ Where the lower end of the trough is drowned by the sea it forms a deep steep-side inlet called *'Fiord'* as on the Norwegian and South Chilean Coasts.

U-shaped valley
▷ When a glacier is flowing through a valley in a mountainous region, the sides of the valley get eroded. Ice causes friction on the sides of the valley.
▷ As the erosion of the sides is greater than that of the floor, a valley is formed with vertical sides and a wide floor. This valley is called a *U-shaped valley*.

Hanging valley
▷ In the mountainous region, many tributaries join the main glacier.
▷ The quantity of ice in a tributary is comparatively smaller. Hence, it causes less friction.
▷ The valley of a tributary is at a higher level than a valley of the main glacier, the valley of the tributary appears to be hanging. That is why, such a valley is called a *hanging valley*.

Moraine

⇨ The material transported and deposited by a glacier is known as *moraine*.
⇨ Moraines are made up of pieces of rocks that are shattered by frost action and are brought down the valley.

Moraines are of the following types

(1) lateral moraine, (2) medial moraine (3) terminal moraine and (4) ground moraines.

⇨ After a glacier has melted, different land forms of deposition are seen.
⇨ The oval-shaped hills of lesser height are called *drumlins*.
⇨ Zig-zag hills, with many steep slopes, made up of long stretches of sand and gravel are called *eskers*.

Land forms created by the action of wind

Mushroom rock

⇨ The wind blowing in desert regions erodes the rock near the ground surface to a great extent. At the same time, the upper part of the rock gets eroded to a lesser extent.
⇨ As this is a continuous process, the foot of the rock becomes narrow.
⇨ The top portion of the rock then looks like an umbrella. This land form is called a *mushroom rock*.

Sand dunes

⇨ Sand gets transported from one place to another along with the wind.
⇨ At a spot where the wind meets an obstruction or where the speed of the wind reduces, dunes are formed out of the sand which gets deposited.
⇨ The side of the dune facing the wind has a gentle slope and the opposite side has a steep slope.
⇨ Because of the slow speed of the wind, the sand on the gentle slope gets carried to the top and comes down the steep slope on the other side. Sand dunes gradually move forward in this manner.

Barkhan

⇨ The fine sand particles carried by the wind get deposited when the speed of the wind is reduced forming crescent shaped dunes. Such hills are called *barkhans*.

Loess

⇨ *Loess is a soil* finer than sand.
⇨ *Loess is a silt* transported by the wind from the desert regions and deposited much further way.
⇨ Loess transported from the desert regions of Central Asia has been deposited in layers in China. The plain they form is known as the *Loess plain*.

Groundwater

⇨ Some water from the rainfall received on the earth's surface seeps through the ground.

⇨ This water trickles down until it reaches an impervious rock.

⇨ Water accumulated under the ground surface in this manner, is called *ground water*.

⇨ Some rocks on the earth's surface are porous and some have cracks or joints. Water seeps in through these pores or joints.

⇨ Groundwater gushes out in the form of *springs*.

Land forms created by the actions of groundwater

Sink holes

⇨ Water on the ground surface seeps through limestone. Some portion of the limestone dissolves in that water. If this process takes place continuously, it makes holes in these rocks.

⇨ As this process continues over a number of years, these holes get enlarged. These holes are called *sink holes*.

Caves

⇨ In limestone region, water goes very deep through sink holes.

⇨ If there is a layer of impervious and hard rock underneath, water flows horizontally on the impervious rock instead of going deeper.

⇨ Hence, soft rocks get eroded and a *cave* is formed.

Stalactites and stalagmites

⇨ Inside the cave created by groundwater under the ground surface in a limestone region, water is always seeping through the roof. This water contains *calcium carbonate*.

⇨ As the seeping water evaporates, some of the calcium carbonate, it contains, is deposited on the cave's roof. This deposition continues to grow very slowly. Hence a column is seen growing from the roof towards the floor. It is called a *stalactite*.

⇨ The water dripping on the floor of the cave also evaporates leaving behind calcium carbonate which accumulates over a period of time.

⇨ A column then starts growing from the floor to the roof. This column which grows upwards is called a *stalagmite*.

⇨ Stalactites and stalagmites are observed in the Parner Taluka of Ahmad-nagar district, in Bastar District in Chhattisgarh and also in the Karst region of former Yugoslavia now Serbia and Montenegro.

Land forms created by the actions of sea waves

Sea Cliff

⇨ The base of the rocks on the coast get eroded because of the impact of the ocean waves and notches develop in these rocks.

⇨ The crest of the rock overhangs the notch. These notches in the rocks gradually extend landwards over a period of time. Then the crest falls and a steep *cliff*, which has receded away from the sea is formed.

Sea cave
⇨ Rocks on the coast have many cracks. They become wider and wider with the impact of the waves, creating small caves. They are called sea caves.
⇨ Such sea cliffs and sea caves are observed at Shrivandhan, Ratnagiri, Malvan, Vengurle etc.

Beach
⇨ The fine sand and other material that flows along with the waves get deposited in a direction parallel to the sea coast.
⇨ This deposition of sand is called a *beach*.
⇨ There are extensive beaches in the coastal regions of the states of Maharashtra, Goa, Kerala, Tamil Nadu, Odisha and West Bengal in India and in other countries like Bangladesh and Canada.

Sand bar
⇨ A deposition of sand which results in a long, narrow embankment in the sea near the coast is called a *sand bar*.

Lagoon
⇨ A shallow lake is formed between the sand and the sea coast. It is called a *lagoon*. Such a lake is called *Kayal* in Kerala.

21. World Around Us
Major Geographical Findings
⇨ *Amundsen* – He discovered the South Pole in 1912.
⇨ *Neil Armstrong* – He was the first person to set foot on the moon on July 21, 1969.
⇨ *Columbus* – He discovered West Indies in 1492 and South America in 1498.
⇨ *Copernicus* – He discovered the Solar System in 1540.
⇨ *Edmund Hillary* – Joint & Tenzing Norgay- They were the first people to reach the summit of Mt. Everest.
⇨ *Kepler* – He discovered the Laws of Planetary Motion in 1609.
⇨ *Lindbergh* – He performed the first solo-flight across the Atlantic in 1927 from New York to Paris.
⇨ *Magellan*– He commanded the first expedition in 1519 to sail a round the world.
⇨ *Marco Polo*– He explored China, India, South-Eastern countries and published the record of his various explorations. He was the first European to visit China.
⇨ *Robert Peary*– He was the first person to reach the North Pole, in 1909.
⇨ *Vasco da Gama (Portuguese)*– He circled the Cape of Good Hope and discovered the sea route to India in 1498.

Miscellaneous

1. Major Seas

Sea	Area	Sea	Area
South China	(2,974,600 sq km)	Hudson Bay	(730,100 sq km)
Caribbean	(2,515,900 sq km)	East China	(664,600 sq km)
Mediterranean	(2,510,000 sq km)	Andaman	(564,900 sq km)
Bering	(2,261,100 sq km)	Black Sea	(507,900 sq km)
Gulf of Mexico	(1,507,600 sq km)	Red Sea	(453,000 sq km)
Arabian Sea	(1,498,320 sq km)	Baltic Sea	(4, 22,300 sq km)
Sea of Okhotsk	(1,392,100 sq km)	Gulf of St. Lawrence	(2, 37,760 sq km)
Sea of Japan (East Sea)	(1,012,900 sq km)	Gulf of California	(1, 62,000 sq km)

2. Important Rivers

River	Length	River	Length
Amazon, South America	6,437 km	Amur, Asia	4,416 km
Chang Jiang (Yangtze), Asia	6,380 km	Congo, Africa	4,370 km
Mississippi, North America	5,971 km	Mackenzie-Peace, North America	4,241 km
Yenisey-Angara, Asia	5,536 km	Mekong, Asia	4,184 km
Huang (Yellow), Asia	5,464 km	Niger, Africa	4,171 km
The Ganga, Asia	2,510 km	The Ganga, Asia	2,510 km
Nile, Africa	6,825 km	The Brahmaputra, Asia	2900 km

3. Important Lakes

Lake	Area	Lake	Area
Great Bear, North America	31,300 sq km	Caspian Sea, Asia-Europe	371,000 sq km
Aral Sea, Asia	30,700 sq km	Superior, North America	82,100 sq km
Malawi, Africa	28,900 sq km	Victoria, Africa	69,500 sq km

Great Slave, Canada	28,568 sq km	Huron, North America	59,600 sq km
Erie, North America	25,667 sq km	Michigan, North America	57,800 sq km
Winnipeg, Canada	24,387 sq km	Tanganyika, Africa	32,900 sq km
Ontario, North America	19,529 sq km	Baikal, Asia	31,500 sq km
Balkhash, Kazakhstan	18,300 sq km		

4. Important Mountain Peaks

Mountain	Hight	Mountain	Hight
Makalu I	27,765 ft (8,462 m) Nepal	Mount Everest	29,035 ft (8,850 m) Nepal/China
Cho Oyu	26,906 ft (8,201 m) Nepal	Qogir (K2)	28,250 ft (8,611 m) Pakistan
Dhaulagiri	26,794 ft (8,167 m) Nepal	Kanchenjunga	28,169 ft (8,586 m) Nepal
Manaslu I	26,758 ft (8,156 m) Nepal	Lhotse	27,920 ft (8,501 m) Nepal
Nanga Parbat	26,658 ft (8,125 m) Pakistan	Annapurna I	26,545 ft (8,091 m) Nepal

5. Important Plateaus

Plateau	Altitude	Plateau	Altitude
Tibetan Plateau	4,500 m	Plateau of Madagascar	2,876 m
Deccan Plateau	600 m	Plateau of Alaska	6,194 m
Arabian Plateau	900 m	Plateau of Bolivia	3,750 m
Plateau of Brazil	2,891 m	Great Basin Plateau	2500-3300 m
Plateau of Mexico	1,219 m	Colorado Plateau	1,585 m
Plateau of Colombia	1,219 m		

6. Major Islands

Island	Area	Island	Area
Greenland	2,175,600 sq km	Ellesmere	196,200 sq km
New Guinea	792,500 sq km	Celebes	178,650 sq km
Borneo	725,500 sq km	New Zealand (south)	151,000 sq km
Madagascar	587,000 sq km	Java	126,700 sq km

Baffin	507,500 sq km	New Zealand (north)	114,000 sq km
Sumatra	427,300 sq km	Newfoundland	108,900 sq km
Honshu	227,400 sq km	Great Britain	218,100 sq km
Australia	7,617.930 sq km	Victoria	217,300 sq km

7. Important Canals

Canal	Location
Panama Canal	This canal extends upto 58 km and connects the Atlantic Ocean and the Pacific Ocean. It was opened up in 1914.
Suez Canal	This canal is 169 km long and it connects the Mediterranean Sea and the Red Sea.
Kiel Canal	It is 98 km long and connects the North Sea and the Baltic Sea, between London and Baltic ports.

8. Major Gulfs

Gulf	Area	Gulf	Area
Gulf of California	1,62,000 sq km	Gulf of Mexico	1,500,000 sq km
Persian Arabian Gulf	51,000 sq km	Gulf of St. Lawrence	2,50,000 sq km
English Channel	75,000 sq km	Gulf of Hudson	3,861,400 sq km

9. Important Straits

Name	Joins	Location
Malacca Strait	Andaman Sea & South China Sea	Indonesia – Malaysia
Palk Strait	Palk Bay & Bay of Bengal	India-Sri Lanka
Sunda Strait	Java Sea & Indian Ocean	Indonesia
Bab-el-Mandeb Strait	Red Sea & Gulf of Aden	Yemen-Djibouti
Bering Strait	Bering Sea & Chuksi Sea	Alaska-Russia
Dover strait	English Channel & North Sea	England-France
Florida Strait	Gulf of Mexico and Atlantic Ocean	USA-Cuba
Gibraltar Strait	Mediterranean Sea & Atlantic Ocean	Spain-Morocco
Magellan strait	Pacific and South Atlantic Ocean	Chile

10. Countries

There are about 196 countries in the world.

Country	Capital	Official Name	Continent	Language	Currency
Afghanistan	Kabul	Islamic Emirate of Afghanistan	Asia	Pushtu Dari	Afghani
Albania	Tirana	Republic of Albania	Europe	Albanian	Lek
Algeria	Algiers	Democratic People's Republic of Algeria	Africa	Arabic, French	Dinar
Andorra	Andorre La Vieille	Principality of Andorra	Europe	Catalan	French Franc, Spanish Peseta
Angola	Luanda	People's Republic of Angola	Africa	Portuguese	re-adjusted Kwanza
Antigua Barbuda	St.John's	Antigua and Barbuda	Caribbean Sea	English	East Caribbean Dollar US
Argentina	Buenos Aires	Argentine Republic	South America	Spanish	Peso
Armenia	Yerevan	Republic of Armenia	Asia	Armenian	the Dram
Australia	Canberra	Commonwealth of Australia	Australia	English	Australian Dollar
Ashmore & Cartier Islands	Kingston (Administrative Centre)	(Territories under Australia in the Indian Ocean)	Indian Ocean	English	Australian Dollar
Christmas Island	Kingston (Administrative Centre)	(Territories under Australia in the Indian Ocean)	Indian Ocean	English	Australian Dollar
Cocos (Keeling) Islands	Kingston (Administrative Centre)	(Territories under Australia in the Indian Ocean)	Indian Ocean	English	Australian Dollar
Herd & Mcdonald Islands	Kingston (Administrative Centre)	(Territories under Australia in the Indian Ocean)	Indian Ocean	English	Australian Dollar
Norfolk Islands	Kingston (Administrative Centre)	(Territories under Australia in the Indian Ocean)	Indian Ocean	English	Australian Dollar

Coral Sea Islands	Kingston (Administrative Centre)	(Territories under Australia in the Indian Ocean)	Pacific Ocean	English	Australian Dollar
Australian Antarctic Territory	Kingston (Administrative Centre)	(Territories under Australia in the Indian Ocean)	Antarctica	English	Australian Dollar
Austria	Vienna	Republic of Austria	Europe	German	Euro Schilling
Azerbaijan	Baku	Azerbaijan Republic	Asia	Azeri	Manat
The Bahamas	Nassau	Commonwealth of the Bahamas	Atlantic Ocean	English	Bahamian Dollar
Bahrain	Manama	State of Bahrain	Asia	Arabic, English	Dinar, Bahraini
Bangladesh	Dhaka	People's Republic of Bangladesh	Asia	Bangla	Taka
Barbados	Bridgetown	Barbados	Atlantic Ocean	English	Barbados Dollar
Belarus Byelorussia	Minsk	Republic of Belarus	Europe	Belorussian	Ruble
Belgium	Brussels	Kingdom of Belgium	Europe	Flemish (Dutch), French, German	Euro
Belize	Belmopan	Belize	Central America	English	Belize Dollar
Benin	Porto-Novo	Republic of Benin	Africa	French	Franc
Bhutan	Thimphu	Kingdom of Bhutan	Asia	Dzongkha	Ngultrum
Bolivia	La Paz; Sucre	Republic of Bolivia	South America	Aymara Spanish, Quechua	The Boliviano
Bosnia-Herzegovina	Sarajevo	Republic of Bosnia - Herzegovina	Europe	Serbo-Croatian	Conv.Mark
Botswana	Gaborone	Republic of Botswana	Africa	English	Pula
Brazil	Brazilia	Federative Republic of Brazil	South America	Portuguese	Real
Brunei	Bander Seri Bagawan	State of Brunei Darussalam	Asia	Malay, Chinese	Brunei Dollar
Bulgaria	Sofia	Republic of Bulgaria	Europe	Bulgarian	Lev

Burkina Faso	Ouagadougou	Burkina Faso	Africa	French	Franc
Burundi	Bujumbura	Republic of Burundi	Africa	Kirundi, French	Burundi Franc
Cambodia	Phnom-Penh	Kingdom of Cambodia	Asia	Khmer	Rial
Cameroon	Yaounde	Republic of Cameroon	Africa	French, English	Franc CFA
Canada	Ottawa	Canada	North America	French, English	Canadian Dollar
Cape Verde	Praia	Republlic of Cape Verde	Africa	Crioulo	Escudo
Central African Republic	Bangui	Central African Republic	Africa	French	Franc
Chad	N'Djamena	Republic of Chad	Africa	Arabic, French	Franc
Chile	Santiago	Republic of Chile	South America	Spanish	Peso
China	Beijing	People's Republic of China	Asia	Chinese (Mandarin)	Yuan
Hong Kong	Victoria	Chinese Territory in China Sea	Asia	English, Chinese	Hong Kong Dollar
Colombia	Bogota	Republic of Colombia	South America	Spanish	Peso
The Comoros	Moroni	Federal Islamic Republic of the Comoros	Africa	Comoran	Comoran Franc
Congo Formerly Zaire	Kinshasa	Democratic Republic of the Congo	Africa	French	Congolese Franc
Costa Rica	San Jose	Republic of Costa Rica	Central America	Spanish	Colon
Cote d'Ivoire (Ivory coast)	Abidjan	Republic of Cote d'Ivoire	Africa	French	Franc
Croatia	Zagreb	Republic of Croatia	Europe	Croatian	Kuna
Cuba	Havana	Republic of Cuba	Caribbean Sea	Spanish	Peso
Cyprus	Nicosia	Republic of Cyprus	Mediterra-nean Sea	Greek, Turkish	Cyprus Pound
Turkish Cyprus	Nicosia North	Turkish Republic of Northern Cyprus	Mediterr-anean Sea	Turkish	Turkish Lira
Czech Republic	Prague	Ceska Republica	Europe	Czech	Koruna

Denmark	Copenhagen	Kingdom of Denmark	Europe	Danish	Krone
Faeroe Islands	Rorshavn	Territories under Denmark	Atlantic Ocean in between Atlantic and Arctic Oceans	Danish	Krone
Greenland	Nuuk	Territories under Denmark	Atlantic Ocean in between Atlantic and Arctic Oceans	Danish and Greenlandic	Krone
Djibouti	Djibouti	Republic of Djibouti	Africa	Arabic	Djibouti Franc
Dominica	Roseau	Commonwealth of Dominica	Caribbean Sea	French patois, Eng.	East Caribbean Dollar
Dominican Republic	Santo Domingo	Dominican Republic	Caribbean Sea	Spanish	Peso Oro
Ecuador	Quito	Republic of Ecuador	South Ameirca	Spanish	Sucre
Egypt	Cairo	Arab Republic of Egypt	Africa	Arabic	Egyptian Pound
El Salvador	San Salvador	Republic of El Salvador	Central America	Spanish	Colon
Equatorial Guinea	Malabo	Republic of Equatorial Guinea	Africa	Spanish	Franc
Eritrea	Asmara	State of Eritrea	Africa	Tigrigna	Nakfa
Estonia	Tallinn	Republic of Estonia	Europe	Estonian	Kroon
Ethiopia	Addis Ababa	Federal Democratic Republic of Ethiopia	Africa	Amharic	Birr
Fiji	Suva	Republic of Fiji	South Pacific Ocean	English	Fijian Dollar
Finland	Helsinki	Republic of Finland	Europe	Finnish, Swedish	Markka
France	Paris	French Republic	Europe	French	Euro
French Guayana	Caine	French Republic	South America	French	Euro
Pappeet	Pappeet	French Republic	Pacific Ocean	French	Euro
French Southern and Arabic Lands		French Republic	Antarctic Indian Ocean	French	Euro

Guadeloupe	Basse-Terre	French Republic	Caribbean Sea	French	Euro
Martinique	Fort-de-France	French Republic	Caribbean Sea	French	Euro
Mayotte	Dzaoudzic	French Republic	Indian Ocean (Mozambic Channel)	French	Euro
New Caledonia	Naumia	French Republic	Pacific Ocean	French	Euro
Reunion	Saint Dennis	French Republic	Indian Ocean	French	Euro
Saint Pierre & Miquelon	Saint - Pierre	French Republic	Atlantic Ocean	French	Euro
Wallis Futuna Islands	Matta-Uttu	French Republic	Pacific Ocean	French	Euro
Gabon	Libreville	Gabonese Republic	Africa	French	Franc
The Gambia	Banjul	Republic of the Gambia	Africa	English	Dalasi
Georgia	Tbilisi	Republic of Georgia	Asia	Georgian	The Lari
Germany	Berlin	Federal Republic of Germany	Europe	German	Euro
Ghana	Accra	Republic of Ghana	Africa	English	New Cedi
Greece	Athens	Hellenic Republic	Europe	Greek	Drachma
Grenada	St.Georges	State of Grenada	Caribbean Sea	English	East Caribbean, Dollar
Guatemala	Guatemala City	Republic of Guatemala	Central America	Spanish	Quetzal
Guinea	Conakry	Republic of Guinea	Africa	French	Franc
Guinea-Bissau	Bissau	Republic of Guinea - Bissau	Africa	Portuguese	CFA Franc
Guyana	Georgetown	Co-operative Republic of Guyana	South America	English	Guyana Dollar
Haiti	Port-au-Prince	Republic of Haiti	Caribbean Sea	French	Gourde
Honduras	Tegucigalpa	Republic of Honduras	Central America	Spanish	Lempira
Hungary	Budapest	Republic of Hungary	Europe	Hungarian	Forint

Countries	Area	Countries	Area
Algeria	2,381,740 km²	Russia	17,075,200 km²
Democratic Republic of the Congo	2,345,410 km²	Canada	9,984,670 km²
Mexico	1,972,550 km²	United States	9,631,418 km²
Saudi Arabia	1,960,582 km²	China	9,596,960 km²
Indonesia	1,919,440 km²	Brazil	8,511,965 km²
Sudan	1,886,068 km²	Australia	7,686,850 km²
Libya	1,759,540 km²	India	3,287,590 km²
Iran	1,648,000 km²	Argentina	2,766,890 km²
Mongolia	1,564,116 km²	Kazakhstan	2,717,300 km²
Peru	1,285,220 km²	Chad	1,284,000 km²

Largest Countries – By Population

Country	Population	Country	Population
Pakistan	173,593,000	China	1,341,335,000
Nigeria	158,423,000	India	1,224,614,000
Bangladesh	148,692,000	United States	310,384,000
Russia	142,958,000	Indonesia	239,781,000
Japan	126,536,000	Brazil	194,946,000

Richest Countries (GNP in US dollars)

Country	GNP	Country	GNP
Iceland	37,920	Luxembourg	56,380
Japan	37,050	Norway	51,810
Sweden	35,840	Switzerland	49,600
Ireland	34,310	USA	41,440
UK	33,630	Denmark	40,750

Poorest Countries (GNP in US dollars)

Country	GNP	Country	GNP
Tanzania	720	Timor-Leste	400
Yemen	745	Malawi	596
Burundi	753	Somalia	600
Afghanistan	800	Democratic Republic of the Congo	675
Guinea-Bissau	856	Ethiopia	859

Countries with Most Urbanisation (as per the 2008 census)

Country	Urbanisation Percentage	Country	Urbanisation Percentage
Vatican City	100%	Singapore	100%
Gibraltar	100%	Nauru	100%
Cayman Islands	100%	Monaco	100%
Bermuda	100%	Macau	100%
Anguilla	100%	Hong Kong	100%

Countries with Least Urbanisation (according to the 2008 census)

Country	Urbanisation Percentage	Country	Urbanisation Percentage
Liechtenstein	14%	Rwanda	18%
Uganda	13%	Nepal	17%
Trinidad and Tobago	13%	Ethiopia	17%
Papua New Guinea	12%	Niger	16%
Burundi	10%	Sri Lanka	15%
Wallis and Futuna	0%	Montserrat	14%
Tokelau	0%	Pitcairn Islands	0%

11. Highest Life Expectancy (as per the 2011 census)

Country	Life Expectancy	Country	Life Expectancy
Australia	81.8 years	Monaco	89.73 years
Italy	81.77 years	San Marino	83.01 years
Canada	81.38 years	Andorra	82.43 years
France	81.19 years	Japan	82.25 years
Spain	81.17 years	Singapore	82.14 years

Lowest Life Expectancy (2011)

Country	Lowest Life Expectancy	Country	Lowest Life Expectancy
Sierra Leone	41.24 years	Swaziland	31.9 years
Liberia	41.8 years	Angola	38.2 years
Djibouti	43.37 years	Zambia	38.63 years
Malawi	43.82 years	Lesotho	40.4 years

Central African Republic	44.5 years	Mozambique	41.18 years

12. National Emblems of Different Countries

Country	National Emblem	Country	National Emblem
Australia	Kangaroo	Bangladesh	Water Lily
Barbados	Head of a Trident	Belgium	Lion
Canada	White Lily	Chile	Candor & Huemul
Denmark	Beach	Dominica	Sisserou Parrot
France	Lily	Germany	Corn Flower
Guyana	Canje Pheasant	Hong Kong	Bauhinia (Orchid Tree)
India	Lioned Capital	Iran	Rose
Ireland	Shamrock	Israel	Candelabrum
Italy	White Lily	Ivory Coast	Elephant
Japan	Chrysanthemum	Lebanon	Cedar Tree
Luxembourg	Lion with Crown	Mongolia	The Soyombo
Netherlands	Lion	New Zealand	Southern Cross, Kiwi, Fern
Norway	Lion	Pakistan	Crescent
Papua New Guinea	Bird of paradise	Spain	Eagle
Senegal	Baobab Tree	Sierra Leone	Lion
Sri Lanka	Lion	Sudan	Secretary Bird
Syria	Eagle	Turkey	Crescent & Star
U.K.	Rose	U.S.A.	Golden Rod

13. National Monuments of Some Countries

Country	Monuments
Australia	Opera House (Sydney)
China	The Great Wall of China
Denmark	Kinder disk
Egypt	Pyramid
France	Eiffel Tower (Paris)
India	The Taj Mahal (Agra)
Italy	Leaning Tower of Pisa

Japan	Imperial Palace
Malaysia	Tugu Negara
Russia	Kremlin (Moscow)
USA	Statue of Liberty (New York)

14. Parliaments of Different Countries

Country	Partiament	Country	Partiament
Afghanistan	Shora	Denmark	Folketing
Andorra	General Council	Dominica	House of Assembly
Albania	People's Assembly	Ecuador	National Congress
Azerbaijan	Melli Majlis	El Salvador	Legislative Assembly
Algeria	National Popular Assembly	East Timor	Constituent Assembly
Angola	National Popular Assembly	Ethiopia	Federal Council and House of Representative
Argentina	National Congress	Egypt	People's Assembly
Australia	Federal Parliament	Fiji Islands	Senate & House of Representative
Austria	National Assembly	France	National Assembly
Bahamas	General Assembly	Finland	Eduskusta (Parliament)
Bahrain	Consultative Council	Germany	Lower House and Upper House
Bangladesh	Jatiya Sangshad	Guyana	National Assembly
Belize	National Assembly	Greece	Chamber of Deputies
Bhutan	Tsogdu	Hungry	National Assembly
Bolivia	National Congress	Iceland	Althing
Brazil	National Congress	India	Sansad
Brunei	National Assembly	Indonesia	People's Consultative

Botswana	National Assembly	Iran	Majlis
Britain	Parliament (House of Commons & House of Lords)	Iraq	National Assembly
Bulgaria	National Assembly	Israel	Knesset
Cambodia	National Assembly	Italy	Chamber of Deputies and Senate
Congo	Rep. of National Legislative Council	Nepal	Rashtriya Panchayat
Colombia	Congress	Netherlands	The Staten General
Canada	House of Commons and Assembly Senate	New Zealand	Parliament(House of Representatives)
China	National People's Congress	Oman	Monarchy
Comoros	Legislative Council and Senate	Pakistan	National Assembly & Senate
Chile	Chamber of Deputies and Senate	Paraguay	Senate & Chamber of Deputies
Costa Rica	Legislative Council and Senate	Philippines	The Congress
Croatia	Sabor	Papua New Guinea	National Parliament
Cuba	National Assembly of People's Power	Poland	Sejm
Czech Republic	Chamber of Deputies and Senate	Romania	Great National Assembly
Japan	Diet	Russia	Duma & Federal Council
Jordan	National Assembly	Senegal	National Assembly

Korea (North)	Supreme People's Assembly	Seychelles	People's Assembly
Korea (South)	National Assembly	South Africa Rep.	House of Assembly
Kuwait	National Assembly	Spain	Cortes Generales
Laos	People's Supreme Assembly	Sweden	Riksdag
Lebanon	National Assembly	Saudi Arabia	Majlis Al-Shura
Lesotho	National Assembly and Senate	Sudan	Majlis Watahi
Lithuania	Seimas	Switzerland	Federal Assembly
Luxembourg	Chamber of Deputies	Syria	People's Council
Libya	General People's Congress	Turkey	Grand National Assembly
Malaysia	Dewan Rakyat and Dewan Negara	USA	Congress
Maldives	Majlis	Vietnam	National Assembly
Madagascar	National People's Assembly	Venezuela	National Congress
Mongolia	The Great Khural	Yugoslavia	Federal Assembly
Mozambique	National Assembly	Zambia	National Assembly
Myanmar	People's Assembly		

15. Major Political Parties of the World

Country	Political	Country	Political
Australia	Liberal Party, Labour Party	France	Socialist Party, National Front, Union for French Democracy
China	Chinese Communist Party	USA	Democratic Party, Republican Party

India	Indian National Congress, Bharatiya Janata Party	Sri Lanka	Freedom Party, United National Party
Bangladesh	Bangladesh National Party, Awami League, Jatiya Party	UK	Labour Party, Conservative Party, Liberal Democratic Party
Russia	Liberal Democratic Party, Communist Party	Pakistan	Muslim League, Pakistan People's Party
Nepal	Nepali Congress, Nepali Communist Party		

16. Most Populated Cities of the World

City	Population	City	Population
Tokyo, Japan	32,450,000	Tehrãn, Iran	7,380,000
Seóul, South Korea	20,550,000	Bangkok, Thailand	7,221,000
Mexico City, Mexico	20,450,000	Chicago, USA	6,945,000
New York City, USA	19,750,000	Bogotá, Colombia	6,834,000
Mumbai, India	19,200,000	Hyderabad, India	6,833,000
Jakarta, Indonesia	18,900,000	Chennai, India	6,639,000
Sáo Paulo, Brazil	18,850,000	Essen, Germany	6,559,000
Delhi, India	18,680,000	Ho Chi Minh City, Vietnam	6,424,519
Õsaka/Kobe, Japan	17,350,000	Hangzhou, China	6,389,000
Shanghai, China	16,650,000	Hong Kong, China	6,097,000
Manila, Philippines	16,300,000	Lahore, Pakistan	6,030,000
Los Angeles, USA	15,250,000	Shenyang, China	5,681,000
Kolkata, India	15,100,000	Changchun, China	5,566,000
Moscow, Russian Fed.	15,000,000	Bangalore, India	5,544,000
Cairo, Egypt	14,450,000	Harbin, China	5,475,000
Lagos, Nigeria	13,488,000	Chengdu, China	5,293,000
Buenos Aires, Argentina	13,170,000	Santiago, Chile	5,261,000
London, United Kingdom	12,875,000	Guangzhou, China	5,162,000

Beijing, China	12,500,000	St. Petersburg, Russian Fed.	5,132,000
Karachi, Pakistan	11,800,000	Kinshasa, DRC	5,068,000
Dhaka, Bangladesh	10,979,000	Baghdād, Iraq	4,796,000
Rio de Janeiro, Brazil	10,556,000	Jinan, China	4,789,000
Tianjin, China	10,239,000	Houston, USA	4,750,000
Paris, France	9,638,000	Toronto, Canada	4,657,000
Istanbul, Turkey	9,413,000	Lima, Peru	7,443,000

17. Major Industrial Countries of the World

Industries	Countries
Iron & Steel	USA, Russia, Japan, Germany, UK, France, India
Automobile	USA, Japan, Germany
Paper	USA, Canada, Japan, UK, Germany, Sweden, Norway, Finland, Russia, India
Rubber	USA, UK, Germany, France, Netherlands, Australia, Canada, Brazil, Indonesia
Pharmaceuticals	USA, EU, Japan, India
Sugar	Brazil, India, China, Australia, Thailand
Aircraft	USA, EU, France, Brazil
Chemicals	USA, Germany, Russia, UK, Japan, Canada, Australia, India

18. Major Newspapers of the World

Newspaper	Country	Circulation
Yomiuri Shimbun	Japan	14,067
The Asahi Shimbun	Japan	12,121
Mainichi Shimbun	Japan	5,587
Nihon Keizai Shimbun	Japan	4,635
Chunichi Shimbun	Japan	4,512
Bild	Germany	3,867
Sankei Shimbun	Japan	2,757
Canako Xiaoxi (Beijing)	China	2,627
People's Daily	China	2,509
Tokyo Sports	Japan	2,425
The Sun	United Kingdom	2,419

The Chosun Ilbo	South Korea	2,378
USA Today	USA	2,310
The Wall Street Journal	USA	2,107
Daily Mail	UK	2,093
The Joongang Ilbo	South Korea	2,084
The Dong-A Ilbo	South Korea	2,052
Nikkan Sports	Japan	1,965
Hokkaido Shimbun	Japan	1,922
Dainik Jagran	India	1,911
Yangtse Evening Post	China	1,715
Sports Nippon	Japan	1,711
The Nikkan Gendai	Japan	1,686
Times of India	India	1,680
Guangzhou Daily	China	1,650
The Mirror	UK	1,597
Yukan Fuji	Japan	1,559
Shizuoka Shimbun	Japan	1,479
Nanfang City News (Guangzhou)	China	1,410
Dainik Bhaskar	India	1,405
Sankei Sports	Japan	1,368
Hochi Shimbun	Japan	1,354
Yangcheng Evening News (Guangzhou)	China	1,320
Malayala Manorama	India	1,309
Liberty Times	Taiwan	1,300
Thai Rath	Thailand	1,200
New York Times	USA	1,121
Hindustan Times	India	1,108
Chutian Metro Daily (Wuhan)	China	1,084
Gujarat Samachar	India	1,051
Ananda Bazar Patrika	India	1,046
Xinmin Evening News (Shanghai)	China	1,045
Eenadu	India	1,039

Nishi-Nippon Shimbun	Japan	1,025
Kronen Zeitung	Austria	1,009
WAZ Mediengruppe	Germany	1,001
United Daily News	Taiwan	1,000
China Times	Taiwan	1,000
Daily Sports	Japan	999
The Hindu	India	989

19. Major News Agencies

⇨ Reuters
⇨ Associated Press (AP)
⇨ Agence France Presse (AFP)
⇨ United Press International (UPI)
⇨ Deutsche Presse Agentur (DPA)
⇨ Xinhua News Agency
⇨ RIA Novosti (Russian Information Agency)
⇨ Interfax News Agency
⇨ Press Association
⇨ EP (Europa Press)

20. Geographical Epithets

Epithet Sobriquet	Original Name	Epithet Sobriquet	Original Name
Bengal's Sorrow	Damodar River	Land of Kangaroo	Australia
Blue Mountains	Nilgiri Hills	Land of Lilies	Canada
Britain of the South	New Zealand	Land of Morning Calm	Korea
City of the Golden Gate	San Francisco (USA)	Land of Thunderbolt	Bhutan
City of Dreaming Spires	Oxford (UK)	Land of Five Rivers	Punjab, India
City of Magnificent Distance	Washington, DC, USA	Land of Rising Sun	Japan
City of Sky – Scrapers	New York	Yellow River	Huang – Ho
City of Seven Hills	Rome	Land of Midnight Sun	Norway

City of Palaces	Kolkata	Land of Thousand Lakes	Finland
China's Sorrow	Huang - Ho	Land of Maples	Canada
Cockpit of Europe	Belgium	Land of White Elephant	Thailand
Dark Continent	Africa	Mysore Tiger	Tippu Sultan
Eternal City	Rome	Manchester of India	Mumbai
Emerald Island	Ireland	Manchester of Tamil Nadu	Coimbatore
Empire City	New York, U.S.A.	Never Never Land	Prairies of N. Australia
Forbidden City	Lhasa, Tibet	Paradise on Earth	Kashmir Valley (India)
Garden of England	Kent, England	Pearl of the Pacific	Guayaquil Port of Ecuador
Gate of Tears	Bab - el - mandeb, Jerusalem	Playground of Europe	Switzerland
Garden City	Chicago	Playground of India	Kashmir
Gateway of India	Mumbai	Pearl of the Antilles	Cuba
Gateway of Tamilnadu	Tuticorin	Pillar of Hercules	Gibraltar
Gift of the Nile	Egypt	Pink City	Jaipur
Granite City	Aberdeen, Scotland	Quaker City	Philadelphia, U.S.A.
Great Broadway	New York	Queen of the Adriatic	Venice, Italy
Great Whiteway	Broadway, New York	Queen of the Arabian Sea	Kochi
Granary of South India	Tanjore	Roof of the World	Pamirs, Central Asia
Hearing Pond	Atlantic Ocean	Saint of the Gutters	Mother Teresa
Hermit Kingdom	Korea	Sickman of Europe	Turkey

Holy Land	Palestine	Spice Garden of India	Kerala
Island Continent	Australia	Sugar Bowl of the World	Cuba
Island of Cloves	Zanzibar	Venice of the East	Alappuzha, India
Island of Pearls	Bahrain	Venice of the North	Stockholm, Sweden
Key to Mediterranean	Gibraltar	White City	Belgrade, Yugoslavia
Lady with a lamp	Florence Nightingale	Windy City	Chicago, U.S.A.
Land of Lakes	Scotland	White Man's Grave	Guinea Coast
Land of the Golden Fleece	Australia	World's Bread Basket	Prairies of North America
Land of the Golden Pagoda	Myanmar	World's Loneliest Island	Tristanda Cuntra

21. Important Boundaries around the World

⇨ **Durand Line:** Between Pakistan and Afghanistan, demarcated by Sir Mortimer Durand in 1896.

⇨ **Hindenberg Line:** The line to which the Germans retreated in 1917 during the First World War, defines the boundary between Germany and Poland.

⇨ **Line of Control:** It divides Kashmir between India and Pakistan.

⇨ **Maginot Line:** Boundary between France and Germany.

⇨ **Mannerheim Line:** Drawn by General Mannerheim; fortification on the Russia and Finland border.

⇨ **McMahon Line:** The boundary between India and China as demarcated by Sir Henry McMahon in 1914. China does not recognise this line.

⇨ **Oder Niesse Line:** Boundary between Germany and Poland.

⇨ **Radcliffe Line:** Drawn by Sir Cyril Radcliffe in 1947 as demarcation between India and Pakistan.

⇨ **Seigfrid Line:** Line of fortification drawn by Germany on its border with France.

⇨ **17th Parallel:** The line which defined the boundary between North Vietnam and South Vietnam before the two were united.

⇨ **24th Parallel:** The line which Pakistan claims should be the demarcation between India and Pakistan.

⇨ **38th Parallel:** Boundary between North Korea and South Korea.

⇨ **49th Parallel:** Boundary between USA and Canada.

22. Races and People

Race is a classification system used to categorise humans into large and distinct populations or groups by heritable phenotypic characteristics (physical appearances), geographic ancestry, culture, history, language, ethnicity and social status. In the early twentieth century, the term was often used, in a taxonomic sense, to denote genetically differentiated human populations defined by phenotype.

23. Great Races of the World

Scientific racism of the late 19th and early 20th centuries divided mankind into three "great races", *the Caucasoid (Whites)*, *the Mongoloid (Yellow)* and **the** *Negroid (Blacks)* in accordance with their own world-view.

The populations of the Indian subcontinent,however were problematic to classify under this scheme. They were assumed to be a mixture of an indigenous *Dravidian race*, tentatively with an '*Australoid*' grouping, with an intrusive *Aryan race*, identified as a sub-race to the *Caucasoid race*. However, some authors also assumed the Mongolic admixture, so that India, for the purposes of scientific racism, presented a complicated mixture of all major types.

Edgar Thurston identified a *Homo Dravida* who had more in common with the *Australian aboriginals* than their *Indo-Aryans*.

The Negroid status of the Dravidians, however remained disputed. In 1898, ethnographer Friedrich Ratzel remarked about the "Mongolian features" of "Dravidians", resulting in his "hypothesis of their (Dravidians) close connection with the population of Tibet" whom he adds "Tibetans may be decidedly reckoned in the Mongol race" In 1899, a journal called "Science" summarised Ratzel's findings over India with, "India is for the author of the History of Mankind, Ratzel", a region where races have been broken up pulverised, and kneaded by conquerors. Doubtless a pre-Dravidian negroid type came first, of low stature and mean physique, though these same are, in India, the result of poor social and economic conditions. The Dravidians succeeded the Negroids, and there may have been Malay intrusions, but Australian affinities are denied. Then succeeded *the Aryans* and *the Mongols.*

In 1900, anthropologist Joseph Deniker said, "The *Dravidian* race is connected with both the Indonesian and Australian... the Dravidian race, which it would be better to call the South Indian Race of India, is prevalent among the peoples of Southern India speaking the Dravidian tongues, and also among the Kols and other people of India... The *Veddhas*... come much nearer to the Dravidian type, which moreover also penetrates among the populations of India, even into the middle valley of the Ganges." Deniker groups the "Dravidians" as a "subrace" under the group of "Curly or Wavy Hair Dark Skin" in which he also includes the *Ethiopian* and the *Australian.*

Also, Deniker mentions that the " The Indian race has its typical representatives among the Afghans, the Rajputs, the Brahmins and most of North India, but it has undergone numerous alterations as it is a consequence of crosses with the Assyriod, Dravidian, Mongol, Turkish, Arab and other races."

According to *Carleton S. Coon* in his book, *The Races of Europe 1939*, he classified the Dravidians as *Caucasoid* due to their Caucasoid skull structure and other physical traits, such as noses, eyes and hair.

24. People and Religions of the World

The world's principal religions and spiritual traditions may be classified into a small number of major groups, although this is by no means a uniform practice. This theory began in the 18th century with the goal of recognising the relative levels of civility in societies.

World Religions by percentage

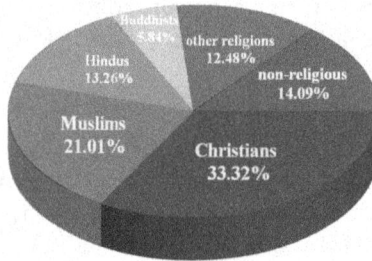

25. Largest Religions of the World

The table below lists religions classified by philosophy; however, religious philosophy is not always the determining factor in local practice. Please note that this table includes heterodox movements as adherents to their larger philosophical category, although this may be disputed by others within that category. For example, Cao Dai is listed because it claims to be a separate category from Buddhism, while Hoa Hao is not, even though they are similar new religious movements. The population numbers below are computed by a combination of census reports, random surveys (in countries where the religions data is not collected in census, for example the United States or France), and self-reported attendance numbers, but results can vary widely depending on the way questions are phrased, the definitions of religion used and the bias of the agencies or organisations conducting the survey. Informal or unorganised religions are especially difficult to count. Some organisations may wildly inflate their numbers.

Religious category	Number of followers (in millions)	Cultural tradition	Founded
Christianity	2,000–2,200[13]	Abrahamic religions	Levant region, 1st century.
Islam	1,570–1,650[14] [15][16]	Abrahamic religions	Arabian Peninsula, 7th century
Hinduism	828–1,000[17]	Indian religions	India.
Buddhism	400–500[18][19][20]	Indian religions	4th century BC, India
Folk religions	Hundreds[nb 1]	Folk religions	Worldwide
Chinese folk religions (including Taoism and Confucianism)	Hundreds[nb 1]	Chinese religions	China.
Shinto	27–65[21]	Japanese religions	Japan.
Sikhism	24–28[22][18]	Indian religions	India.
Judaism	14–18[18]	Abrahamic religions	Levant region.
Jainism	8–12[nb 2]	Indian religions	India, 9th century BC.
Bahá'í Faith	7.6–7.9[23][24]	Abrahamic religions[nb 3]	Iran, 19th century.
Cao ài	1–3[25]	Vietnamese religions	Vietnam.
Cheondoism	3[26]	Korean religions	Korea, 19th century.
Tenrikyo	2[27]	Japanese religions	Japan, 19th century.
Wicca		New religious movements	Britain, 20th century.
Church of World Messianity		Japanese religions	Japan, 20th century.
Seicho-no-Ie		Japanese religions	Japan, 20th century

| Rastafari movement | | New religious movements, Abrahamic religions | Jamaica, 20th century |
| Unitarian Universalism | | New religious movements | United States, 20th century. |

Medium-sized World Religions

The following are some of the medium-sized world religions:

Religious category	Number of followers	Cultural tradition	Founded
Scientology	500,000	New religious movement	United States, 1953
Zoroastrianism	150,000 - 200,000	Iranian religion	Iran, 10th - 15th century BC
Eckankar	50,000 - 500,000	New religious movements	United States, 1973
Satanism	30,000 - 100,000	New religious movement	United States, 1966.
Raëlism	80,000 - 85,000	UFO religion	France, 1974.
Druidry	50,000	Neopaganism	Britain, 18h century.

26. Countries with Their Capital & Currency

Country	Capital	Currency
Afghanistan	Kabul	Afghani
Algeria	Algiers	Dinar
Angola	Luanda	Kwanza
Argentina	Buenos Aires	Argentino Sentavos
Australia	Canberra	Australian Dollar
Austria	Vienna	Shilling
Azerbijan	Baku	Manat
Bahrain	Manama	Bahrain Dinar
Bangladesh	Dhaka	Taka
Belgium	Brussels	Euro
Belarus	Minsk	Belaros Rubbe
Bhutan	Thimphu	Nugultram
Brazil	Brasilia	Real (BRC)

Brunei	Bander Seri Begawan	Brunei Dollar or Ringhit
Bulgaria	Sofia	Lev
Cambodia	Phnom Penh	Rial
Chanada	Ottawa	Dollar
China, Peoples Republic	Beijing	Yuan
Cuba	Havana	Peso
Cyprus	Nicosia	Cyprus Pound
Denmark	Copenhagen	Danish Krone
Egypt	Cairo	Pound
Ethiopia	Adis Ababa	Birr
Fiji	Suva	Dollar
Finland	Helsinki	Euro
France	Paris	Euro
Germany	Berlin	Euro
Ghana	Accra	Cedi
Greece	Athens	Euro
Guatemala	Guatemala City	Quetzal
Hong Kong	Victoria	Dollar
Hungary	Budapest	Florint
Iceland	Reykjavik	Krona
India	New Delhi	Rupee
Indonesia	Jakarta	Rupiah
Iran	Teheran	Rial
Iraq	Baghdad	Iraqui Dinar
Ireland	Dublin	Euro
Israel	Jerusalem	New Shekel
Italy	Rome	Euro
Jamaica	Kingston	Dollar
Japan	Tokyo	Yen
Jordan	Amman	Dinar
Kazakhistan	Almati	Ruble
Kirghizistan	Bishkek	Ruble
Korea (North)	Pyongyang	Won
Korea (South)	Seoul	Won

Kuwait	Kuwait	Dinar
Laos	Vientiane	New Kiplao
Lebanon	Beirut	Pound
Libya	Tripoli	Dinar
Luxembourg	Luxembourg Ville	Euro
Macau	Macau	Pataka
Malaysia	Kuala Lumpur	Ringrit
Maldives, Republic of	Male	Rufia
Mauritius	Port Luis	Rupee
Mexico	Mexico City	New Peso
Mongolia	Ulan Bator	Tugrik
Myanmar	Naypyidaw	Kyat
Mozambique	Maputo	Metical
Nauru	Yaren	Dollar
Nepal	Kathmandu	Rupee
Netherlands	Amsterdam	Euro
New Zealand	Wellington	Dollar
Nigeria	Abuja	Naira
Norway	Oslo	Kroner
Oman	Muscat	Rial
Pakistan	Islamabad	Rupee
Panama	Panama City	Balboa
Philippines	Manila	Peso
Poland	Warsao	Zloty
Portugel	Lisbon	Euro
Qatar	Doha	Riyal
Romania	Bucharest	Lau
Russia	Moscow	Rouble
Saudi Arabia	Riyadh	Riyal
Senegal	Dakar	CFAFranc
Serbia and Montenegro	Belgrade	Dinar
South Africa	Cape Town	Rand
Spain	Madrid	Euro
Singapore	Singapore	Dollar

Sri Lanka	Colombo	Rupee
Syria	Damascus	Pound
Syprus	Nicosia	Pound
Taiwan	Taipei	New Taiwan Dollar
Thailand	Bangkok	Baht
Trinidad & Tobago	Port of Spain	Dollar
Tunisia	Tunis	Dinar
Turkey	Ankara	Lira
United Arab Emirates	Abu Dhabi	Dirham
Uganda	Kampala	Shilling
Ukraine	Kiev	Karbovanets
U.K.	London	Pound Sterling
U.S.A.	Washington D.C.	U.S. Dollar
Venezuela	Caracas	Bolivar
Vietnam	Ho Chi Minh City (Hanoi)	Dong
Yemen	Sena'a	Riyal
Zaire	Kinshasa	Zaire
Zambia	Lusaka	Kwacha
Zimbabwe	Harare	Dollar

27. Wonders of the World
Seven Wonders of the Ancient World
Light House of Alexandra – Ancient island of Pharos (modern day Egypt)

The Colossus of Rhodes – City of Rhodes

The Pyramids of Egypt – Egypt

The Temple of Artemis of Ephesus – Asia Minor, Ephesus

The Hanging Gardens of Babylon – The east bank of Euphrates (modern day Iraq)

The Mausoleum of Halicarnassus- Turkey

Phidias' statue of Zeus- Olympia

Seven Wonders of the Modern World
The Taj Mahal – India

The Great Wall of China – China

Petra – Jordan

Machu Picchu – Peru

Christ Redeemer – Brazil

The Pyramid at Chichen Itza – Mexico

The Roman Colosseum – Italy

28. Countries and their main Produces/ Industries

Afghanistan	Dry and fresh fruits, carpets, wool
Australia	Wood, dairy products, wheat, meat, lead, zinc
Austria	Machinery, textiles, leather goods
Brazil	Coffee
Belgium	Glass, textiles
Chile	Copper Nitrate
Canada	Wheat, newsprint, machinery
China	Silk, tea, rice
Congo	Copper, uranium, cobalt, ivory
Cuba	Sugar, tobacco, cigar
Denmark	Textiles, paper
France	Textile, wine, silk
Germany	Machinery, chemical, iron and steel equipments
Ghana	Coco, gold, coffee
India	Jute, textiles, sugar, spices, tobacco, tea, cement, mica
Indonesia	Sugar, spices, rubber, rice, cinchona, petroleum
Iran	Petroleum, carpets, dry fruits
Iraq	Dates, petroleum
Italy	Mercury, textiles
Japan	Machinery, textiles, toys, silk, automobiles
Kenya	Coffee, tea, meat, sisal, hides and skins, cement, soda ash
Kuwait	Petroleum
Malaysia	Rubber, tin
Netherlands	Machinery, aircraft, electricals
Saudi Arabia	Oil, date
Spain	Lead
Sweden	Matches, timber
Switzerland	Watches, chemicals, electricals
Taiwan	Camphor, rice
UK	Textiles, medicines, machinery, cars

USA	Petroleum, wheat, machinery, coal, automobiles, iron
Russia	Petroleum, wheat, chemicals, heavy machinery
Vietnam	Tin, rice, rubber, teak

29. Famous Sites (India)

Site	Location
Ajanta	Maharashtra
Akabar's Tomb	Agra (U.P.)
Amarnath Cave	Kashmir
Ambar Palace	Jaipur (Rajasthan)
Anand Bhawan	Allahabad (UP)
Bhakra Dam	Punjab
Birla Planetorium	Kolkata (West Bengal)
Island Palace	Udaipur (Rajasthan)
Jagannath Temple	Puri (Orissa)
Jai Stambh (Tower of Victory)	Chittorgarh (Rajasthan)
Jama Masjid	Delhi
Black Pagoda	Konark (Orissa)
Brihadeeshwara Temple	Tanjavur
Brindaban Gardens	Mysore (Karnataka)
Buland Darwaza	Fatehpur Sikri (U.P.)
Char Minar	Hyderabad (Andhra Pradesh)
Chilka Lake	Near Bhubaneswar (Orissa)
Dal Lak	Srinagar (J & K)
Dilwara Temples	Mt. Abu (Rajasthan)
Elephanta Caves	Mumbai (Maharashtra)
Ellora Caves	Aurangabad (Maharashtra)
Gateway of India	Mumbai (Maharashtra)
Golden Temple	Amritsar (Punjab)
Gol Gumbaz	Bizapur (Karnataka)
Hanging Gardens	Mumbai
Hawa Mahal	Jaipur (Rajasthan)
Howrah Bridge	Kolkata (W. Bengal)
Mt. Girnar (Jain Temple)	Junagadh (Gujarat)
Nataraja Temple	Chennai (Tamil Nadu)

Nishat Bagh	Srinagar (J & K)
Padmanabha Temple	Thiruvananthapuram (Kerala)
Palitana	Junagadh (Gujarat)
Panch Mahal	Fatehpur Sikri (U.P.)
Pichola Lake	Udaipur (Rajasthan)
Prince of Wales Museum	Mumbai (Maharashtra)
Qutub Minar	Delhi
Raj Ghat	Delhi
Rashtrapati Bhawan	Delhi
Red Fort	Delhi
Jantar Mantar	New Delhi
Kailash Temple	Ellora (Maharashtra)
Kanya Kumari	Tamil Nadu
Kirti Stambha (Tower of fame)	Chittorgarh (Rajasthan)
Lal Bagh Garden	Bangaluru (Karnataka)
Lingaraj Temple	Bhubaneshwar (Orissa)
Mahakaleshwar	Ujjain (M.P.)
Maheshmukh (Trimurti) Temple	Elephanta Cave (Maharashtra)
Malabar Hills	Mumbai (Maharashtra)
Man Mandir Palace	Gwalior Fort (M.P.)
Marble Rocks	Jabalpur (M.P.)
Marina Beach	Chennai (T.N.)
Minakshi Temple	Madurai (T.N.)
Santa Cruz Air Port	Mumbai (Maharashtra)
Sidi Sayyid Masjid	Ahmedabad (Gujarat)
Shalimar Bagh	Srinagar (J & K)
Shahi Chashma	Srinagar (J & K)
Shanti Van	Delhi
Statue of Gomateshwara	Shravanabelagola, Hasan (Karnataka)
Sun Temple (Black Pagoda)	Konark (Odisha)
Taj Mahal	Agra (Uttar Pradesh)
Tower of Silence	Mumbai (Maharashtra)
Victoria Memorial	Kolkata (W. Bengal)
Victoria Garden	Mumbai (Maharashtra)
Vijay Ghat	Delhi

30. Famous Sites (World)

Site	Location
Al-Aqusa Mosque	Jerusalem (Israel)
Big Ben	London (U.K.)
Bradenberg Gate	Berlin (Germany)
Broadway	New York (U.S.A.)
Brown House	Berlin (Germany)
Buckingham Palace	London (U.K.)
Colossium	Rome (Italy)
Downing Street	London (U.K.)
Eiffel Tower	Paris (France)
Fleet Street	London (U.K.)
Harley Street	London (U.K.)
Hyde Park	London (U.K.)
India House	London (U.K.)
Kaaba	Mecca (Saudi Arabia)
Kremlin	Moscow (Russia)
Leaning Tower	Pisa (Rome)
Louvre	Paris (France)
Merdeka Palace	Jakarta (Indonesia)
Oval	London (U.K.)
Pentagon	Washington (U.S.A.)
Potala	Nanking (China)
Pyramid	Egypt
Red Square	Moscow (Russia)
Scotland Yard	London (U.K.)
Shwe Dragon Pagoda	Yangon (Myanmar)
Sphinx	Egypt
Statue of Liberty	New York (U.S.A.)
Vatican	Rome (Italy)
Wailing Wall	Jerusalem (Israel)
Wall Street	New York (U.S.A.)
Westminster Abbey	London (U.K.)
White Hall	London (U.K.)
White House	Washington (U.S.A.)

31. Changed Names of Cities, States and Countries

Old Name	New Name	Old Name	New Name
Abyssinia	Ethiopia	Ceylon	Sri Lanka
Angora	Ankara	Christina	Oslo
Aurangabad	Sambhaji Nagar	Cochin	Kochi
Banaras	Varanasi	Constantinople	Istanbul
Bangalore	Bangaluru	Dacca	Dhaka
Baroda	Vadodara	Dahomey	Benin
Batavia	Djakarta	Dutch East Indies	Indonesia
Basutoland	Lesotho	Dutch Guiana	Surinam
Bechuanaland	Botswana	Ellice Islands	Tuvalu
Bhatinda	Bathinda	Formosa	Taiwan
Bombay	Mumbai	Gauhati	Guwahati
British Guiana	Guyana	Gold Coast	Ghana
Burma	Myanmar	Holland	The Netherlands
Calcutta	Kolkata	Ivory Coast	Cote D'Ivoire
Calicut	Kozhikode	Jubbulpore	Jabalpur
Cape Canaveral	Cape Kennedy	Jullundur	Jalandhar
Cawnpore	Kanpur	Leopold ville	Kinshasa
Central Provinces	Madhya Pradesh	Madagascar	Malagasy
Madras	Chennai	Malaya	Malaysia
Manchukuo	Manchuria	Mesopotamia	Iraq
New Hebrides	Vanuatu	Nippon	Japan
Northern Rhodesia	Zambia	Nyasaland	Malawi
Ooty	Udhagamandalam	Orissa	Odisha
Panjim	Panaji	Peking	Beijing
Petrograd	Leningrad	Persia	Iran
Palghat	Palakkad	Pondicheri	Puducheri
Poona	Pune	Pretoria	Tshwane
Quilon	Kollam	Rangoon	Yangon
Rhodesia	Zimbabwe	Saigon	Ho Chi Minh City

Salisbury	Harare	Sandwich Islands	Hawaiian Islands
Siam	Thailand	Simla	Shimla
South West Africa	Namibia	Spanish Guinea	Equatorial Guinea
Stalingrad	Volgograd	Tanganyika and Zanzibar	Tanzania
Trichur	Thrissur	Trivandrum	Thiruvanantha-puram
United Provinces	Uttar Pradesh	Upper Volta	Burkina Faso
Uttaranchal	Uttarakhand	Vizagapattam	Visakhapatnam
Zaire	Republic of Congo	Tanjore	Thanjavur

32. Some Tribes and their Homeland (World)

Eskimos: Greenland, North Canada, Alaska, N. Siberia	Lapps: N. Finland, Scandinavian
Koryaks: N. Siberia, Eurassian Tunda, N.E. Asia	Chukchi: N.E. Asia, U.S.S.R., North Siberia
Aleuts: Alaska	Bedouin: Sahara and Middle East
Bushman: Kalahari	Bindibu or Aborigins: Australia
Turregs: Sahara	Gobi Mongols: Gobi
India Tribes: Amazon basin	Orang Asli: Malaysia
Pygmies: Congo basin, Zaire	Masai: East & Central Africa
Hausa: North Nigeria	Aeta: Phillipines
Ainus: Japan	Tapiro: Papua New Guinea
Maoris: New Zealand	Fulani: Western Africa
Hotten tots: Hot tropical Africa	Zulus: South Africa
Ibans: Equatorial rain forest region of South-East Asia	Kirghiz: Asiatic steppes
Kalmuk: Central Asia	Kazakhs: Kazakhistan
Buryak: Central Asia	Red Indian: N. America
Yoakuts: Siberia	Samoyeds: Siberia
Berbers: N . Africa	Guicas: Amazon forest area
Kareus or Meos: Myanmar	Semangs: East Sumatra

Indian Geography

1. Indian Subcontinent

Location

⇨ India is a part of Asia, more specifically, South Asia.

⇨ It is located in the Northern Hemisphere, between 8°4′ and 37°6′ north latitude and 68°7′ and 97°25′ east longitude.

⇨ On the south, India projects into and is bounded by the Indian Ocean.

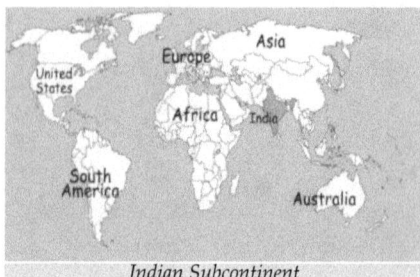

Indian Subcontinent

⇨ South Asia has a total area of about 4.488 million sq. km out of which India has the largest area (3.287 sq. km).

⇨ It occupies 73.2% of total area.

⇨ It accounts for 2.4 per cent of the world's land surface area.

⇨ Our southern boundary extends upto 6°45′ N; latitude in the Bay of Bengal.

Areas and Dimensions

The Union of India is the **seventh largest country** in the world covering an area of 3.28 million sq. km. The mainland measures 3,214 km from north to south and 2,933 km from east to west. The latitudinal and longitudinal extent of India is roughly about 30 degrees. The distance measured from the north to south extremity is around 3,214 km, and that from east to west is 2,933 km.

India has a land frontier of 15,200 km (9,445 miles) and a coastline of 7,517 km (4,671 miles) comprising the mainland, the Lakshadweep Islands, and the Andaman & Nicobar Islands. India's territorial waters extend into the sea to a distance of 12 nautical miles (13.8 mi; 22.2 km) from the coast baseline.

India has eight major mountain ranges having peaks of over 1,000 m (3,281 ft). The Indo-Gangetic plain encompasses an area of 700,000 km² (270,000 sq mi). The *Thar Desert* forms a significant portion of western India and covers an area of about 200,000 km² (77,000 sq mi) to about 238,700 km² (92,200 sq mi). India has around 14,500 km of inland navigable water-ways. The total catchment area of the rivers exceeds 2,528,000 km² (976,000 sq mi). *Mangrove forests* are present all along the Indian coastline and cover a total of 4,461 km² (1,722 sq mi).

Frontiers

The land frontier of the country is about 15, 200 km. The two mountain ranges, the *Sulaiman* and the *Kirthar,* cut it off from the west. Along the North, the great mountain ranges of *Hindu Kush*, Karakoram and the Himalayas, cut it off the countries that lie beyond as the mountains are very high and difficult to cross. The Himalayas and other lofty mountains- Muztagh Ata, Aghil Kunlun Mountains to the north of Kashmir and south the eastern portion of Zaskar mountains to the east of Himachal Pradesh - form India's northern boundary, except in the Nepal region. She is adjoined in the north by China, Nepal and Bhutan. A series of mountain ranges in the east separate India from Burma. Bangladesh, a neighbouring country in the east, is bounded by the Indian States of West Bengal, Assam, Meghalaya, Tripura and Mizoram. In the north-west, Afghanistan and Pakistan lie next to India. The Gulf of Mannar and the Palk Strait separate India from Sri Lanka. The Andaman and Nicobar Islands lie close to Thailand and Indonesia.

Physical Features

India has the following physio-graphic divisions or physical features:

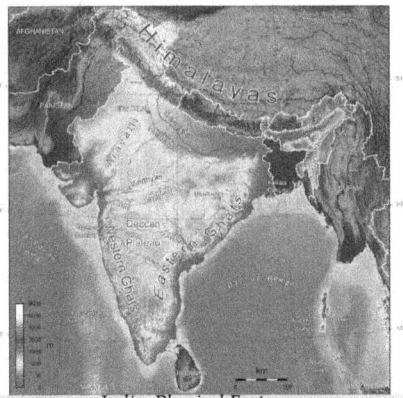
India: Physical Features

⇨ The Himalayan Mountains
⇨ The Northern Plains
⇨ The Peninsular Plateau
⇨ The Indian Desert
⇨ The Coastal Plains
⇨ The Islands

The Himalayan Mountains

The Himalayas are geologically young; structurally fold mountains that stretch along the northern borders of India. They are the loftiest and one of the most rugged mountain barriers of the world. They run in a west-east direction from the Indus River to the Brahmaputra River and form an arc, which covers a distance of about 2,400 km. Their width varies from 400 km in Kashmir to 150 km in Arunachal Pradesh. The altitude of the Himalayas is higher in the eastern half than in the western half.

The Himalayas consist of three parallel ranges in its longitudinal extent.

The Great Inner Himalayas or the 'Himadri': This is the northernmost range and the most continuous range consisting of the loftiest peaks with an average height of 6,000 metres. It contains all the prominent Himalayan peaks, such as Mount Everest (Nepal), Mount Godwin Austin or K2, Kanchenjunga, Mount Makalu and Mount Dhaulagiri.

The Himachal or the Lesser Himalayas: This is the range lying to the south of the Himadri. It forms the most rugged mountain system and the altitude varies between 3,700 and 4,500 metres and the average width is of about 50 km. The Pir Panjal, the DhaulaDhar and the Mahabharat are prominent ranges. This range consists of the famous valley of Kashmir, the Kangra and the Kullu Valley in Himachal Pradesh and other famous hill stations like Shimla, Nainital, Darjeeling, Musoorie, Chail, Ranikhet,Chakrata, etc.

The Shiwaliks are the outermost range of the Himalayas. It is a long chain of narrow and low hills that extend over a width of 10-50 km and have an altitude varying between 900 and 1100 metres. The longitudinal valley located between the Lesser Himalayas and the Shiwaliks are known as Duns. Dehra Dun, Kotli Dun and Patli Dun are some famous Duns. The important ranges here are the Karakoram, the Zanskar, the Patkai, Garo, the Lushai, etc.

The Himalayas have also been divided on the basis of regions from west to east. These divisions have been demarcated by river valleys. For example, the part of the Himalayas lying between the Indus and the Sutlej River is known as the Punjab Himalaya and also as Kashmir and Himachal Himalaya from west to east respectively. The part of the Himalayas lying between Sutlej and the Kali rivers is the Kumaon Himalayas.

The Himalaya

The Kali the and Tista rivers mark off the Nepal Himalayas and the Assam Himalayas is the part lying between the Tista and the Dihang rivers. The Brahmaputra marks the easternmost boundary of the Himalayas. Ahead of the Dihang gorge, the Himalayas bend sharply to the south and spread along the eastern boundary of India. Here they are known as the Purvanchal or the Eastern hills and mountains. The Purvanchal comprises the Patkai hills, the Naga hills, the Manipur hills and the Mizo hills.

The Northern Plains

The Northern Plains, also known as the Indo-Gangetic Plains or the Great Plains has been developed by the three major river systems of India- the Indus, the Ganga and the Brahmaputra. It is spread over an area of about 7 lakh sq.km.

This area is the world's most vast expanse of alluvium formed by the deposition of silt by the rivers. This deposition has made the land here extremely fertile. The flat plains are favourable for irrigation through canals. The area is also rich in ground water sources. Intensive agriculture is practised in the plains and the main crops grown are rice and wheat. Other important crops grown in the region include maize, sugarcane and cotton. Being a highly productive area, it is densely populated.

The Northern Plain is divided into three sections:
▷ *The Punjab-Haryana Plain* is the western part of the Northern Plain. The part of the plains in Haryana is formed by the Yamuna River while

the Punjab part is formed by the Indus and its tributaries–the Jhelum, the Chenab, the Ravi, the Beas and the Sutlej. The Punjab Plains is dominated by the doabs (a land between two rivers).

⇨ *The Gangetic Plain* is the largest part of the the Northern Plain that is spread over a Uttar Pradesh, Bihar and West Bengal.

- The Upper Ganga Plain is formed by the Ganga and its tributaries the Yamuna, the Gomati, and the Ghaghra rivers.
- The Middle Ganga Plain is formed by the Ghaghra, Kosi and the Gandak rivers.
- The Lower Ganga Plain consists mostly of the delta, and here the Ganga gets divided into several channels. This part of the Gangetic Plains is a home to the Sunderbans.

⇨ *The Brahmaputra Plain* lies in Assam, and is formed by the deposits of the Brahmaputra River and its tributaries. It is also known as the Assam Valley.

The Great Plains are also classified into four divisions:

⇨ The Bhabar belt lies next to the foothills of the Himalayas and is made up of boulders and pebbles which have been carried down by the river streams.

⇨ The Terai belt is next to the Bhabar region and is composed of newer alluvium. The region is extremely moist and thickly forested, with a variety of wildlife species. It receives heavy rainfall throughout the year.

⇨ The Bangar belt consists of older alluvium and forms the alluvial terrace of the flood plains.

⇨ The Khadar belt lies in lowland areas after the Bangar belt. It is made up of fresh newer alluvium deposited by the rivers flowing down the plain.

The Peninsular Plateau

The Peninsular plateau is a tableland formed from the Gondwana land, and is made up of the old crystalline, igneous and metamorphic rocks. The plateau has broad and shallow valleys with rounded hills.

This plateau consists of two broad divisions:

⇨ *The Central Highlands* lie to the north of the Narmada river covering a major area of the Malwa plateau. The Vindhyan range is bounded by the Central Highlands on the south and the Aravalis on the northwest. It then gradually merges with the sandy and rocky desert of Rajasthan, towards the west. The Chambal, the Sind, the Betwa and Ken are rivers that flow and drain in this region. The Central

Peninsular Plateau

Highlands are wider in the west but narrower in the east. The eastern parts of this plateau are known as the Bundelkhand and Baghelkhand. Further east, lies the Chotanagpur plateau drained by the Damodar river.

⇨ *The Deccan Plateau* is a triangular landmass that lies to the south of the river Narmada. The Satpura range surrounds its broad base in the north,and the Mahadev, the Kaimur hills and the Maikal range form its eastern extensions. The Deccan Plateau is higher in the west and slopes gently towards the east. The Meghalaya and Karbi-Anglong Plateau is a north eastern extension of the Plateau.

There are three prominent hill ranges from the west to the east:

- the Garo,
- the Khasi and
- the Jaintia Hills

The Peninsular Mountain Ranges: *The Vindhya Range* runs across most of central India, with an average elevation of 9,843 feet. It separates the northern India from southern India. The western end of the range lies in eastern Gujarat, and runs east and north, almost meeting the Ganga at Mirzapur.

⇨ *The Satpura Range* extends from eastern Gujarat near the Arabian Sea coast to the east across Maharashtra, Madhya Pradesh and Chhattisgarh. The height of many peaks here is above 3,281 feet. It is triangular in shape, and runs parallel to the Vindhya Range.

⇨ *The Aravalli Range* is the oldest mountain range in India, located in Rajasthan and running from the north-east to the south-west direction. The northern end of the range extends into Haryana, ending near Delhi. The highest peak in this range is *Guru Shikhar* at Mount Abu with a height of 5,650 feet.

⇨ *The Western Ghats or Sahyadri Mountains* are the western part of India's Deccan Plateau and separate it from a narrow coastal plain along the Arabian Sea. The range runs from the south of the Tapti River near the Gujarat–Maharashtra border and across Maharashtra, Goa, Karnataka, Kerala and Tamil Nadu to the southern tip of the Deccan peninsula. The average elevation is around 3,281 feet. The AnaiMudi in the Anaimalai Hills (8,842 feet) in Kerala is the highest peak in the Western Ghats.

⇨ *The Eastern Ghats (Javadi Hills)* extend from West Bengal to Odisha, Andhra Pradesh and Tamil Nadu. These mountains have been eroded and vivisected by the Godavari, Mahanadi, Krishna and Kaveri. They are not as tall as the Western Ghats, but there average height is about 610 metres and some of its peaks are over 3,281 feet tall. The Jindagada Peak (1657 m), near the Araku Valley of Andhra Pradesh, is the tallest peak in the Eastern Ghats.

⇨ *The Nilgiri hills in Tamil Nadu* lies at the junction of the Eastern and Western Ghats. The highest peak here is Dodda Beta.

The Indian Desert/Thar Desert

The Thar Desert is the world's seventh largest desert. It covers about 200,000 sq. km (77,000 sq mi) to about 238,700 sq. km (92,200 sq mi) area of Western India. Most of it is situated in Rajasthan, covering 61% of its geographic area around.

The Indian Desert

The annual temperatures in this arid region can range from 0°C in the winter to over 50°C during the summer. Chances of rainfall are dicey and patterns are erratic, with patterns ranging from below 120 mm (4.72 inches) in the extreme west to 375 mm (14.75 inches) eastward. It is received from the short July–September southwest monsoon. Water is scarce and is found only at great depths, ranging from 30 to 120 m below the ground level. The soils are generally sandy to sandy-loam in texture. This area has low vegetation cover, having small trees, shrubs, herbs and grasses. They occur in small, scattered clumps.

The Coastal Plains

The Coastal plains of India are the waved platforms and the raised beaches above the water mark. These are mainly floors that emerged from the seas and are adjacent to the land. The Peninsular India Plateau is bordered by the narrow Coastal Plains. Following the surfacing of these lowlands, the sea level fluctuations have brought some important changes in the surface features of the sea shores. The Deccan Plateau in India is also surrounded by the Coastal Plains in the west and the east.

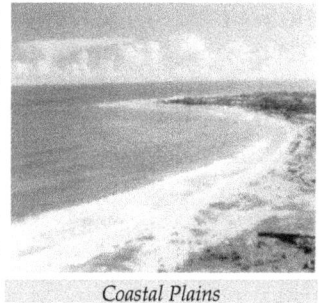
Coastal Plains

The Coastal Plains in the southern region of Kerala are comparatively broad. In some places, the width of the plains gets extended to about 96 km. The off-shore bars are enclosed with lagoons running parallel to the coastal plains in the south of Kerala. Also referred to as Kayals, the lagoons receive water from numerous rivers. The coastal zone located in the western part alongside the Arabian Sea is known in the south of Goa, as *Malabar*, and in the north of Goa as *Konkan*.

Further, there are numerous estuaries in the Coastal Plains. The major ones are the Narmada River and the Tapti River in the state of Gujarat. The plain is also home to natural harbours, such as Marmagao and Mumbai. In the south, the coastal plains merge with the salt water lakes also known as *lagoons*. Spits and sand bars can be found at their mouths. The coast is popular for its serene backwaters. The coastal plains alongside the Bay of Bengal are very extensive and also differ from the plains in the western strip. Fast flowing, small rivers cut across the rocky coastal strip.

The Coastal Plains in India can be divided into two basic types:

The Eastern Coastal Plains

Nestled within the Bay of Bengal and the Eastern Ghats, is the eastern coastal plains, a wide stretch of land having a width of about 120 km. The plains extend from the state of Tamil Nadu in the southern part to the state of West Bengal in the northern region of India. There are several rivers that drain the eastern coastal plains of India. There are also a few river deltas.

These plains experience a temperature of over 30 degrees celsius, characterised by high humidity level. Abundant rainfall is received by this region, amounting to about 1000 mm to 3000 mm annually.

The eastern coastal plains are characterised by numerous rivers, large deltas, fertile and irrigated lands, lagoons, spits and off-shore bars. In places, the plains are bordered with dunes, and mangrove forests also grown here. There is no deep natural harbour in the region except Marmagao (Goa) and Mumbai. Locally, the eastern coastal plain is known as the *Northern Circars* in the region between Krishna and Mahanadi rivers and in regions between the Kaveri and the Krishna River, it is known as the Carnatic.

In the state of Tamil Nadu, the eastern coastal plain is much wider, stretching to about 100 to 120 km of width. The three main divisions into which the eastern coastal plains can be divided are the Andhra Plains, the Utkal Plains and the Tamil Nadu Plains.

The expansive area of the eastern coastal plains that is the three broad divisions, mentioned above can be further divided into *six regions:*

⇨ The Mahanadi Delta in Odisha
⇨ The Southern Andhra Pradesh Plain
⇨ The Krishna Godavari Deltas
⇨ The Kanyakumari or the Kanniyakumari Coast
⇨ The Coromandel Coast in Tamil Nadu
⇨ The Sandy Coastal Regions

The Western Coastal Plains

The western coastal plain of India is situated on a thin strip of land. The plains are nestled by the Arabian Sea and the Western Ghats. Having a length of about 1,400 kilometres and a breadth of 10-80 kilometres, the Western Coastal Plains cover an area of about 64,284 square kilometres. Extending from the state of Gujarat in the northern side to the south in the state of Kerala, the Western Coastal Plains are characterised by many rivers and backwaters and rivers that drain into this area. The rivers that flow through this region form many estuaries in the western coastal plains. The storm activity experienced by these plains is less in comparison to the eastern coastal plains.

Compared with the eastern coastal plains, the western coastal plains are small and can be divided into three parts:

➪ *The Konkan Region–* The northern part of the coast
➪ *The Kanara Region–* Forms a separate transitional zone in between the Malabar coast
➪ *The Malabar Coast–* The southern part of the coast
➪ The Western Coastal Plains also consist of the states of *Karnataka, Maharashtra and Goa.* To the north of the coast lie the *Gulf of Khambat* and the *Gulf of Kutch.*

The Islands

The islands of India are one of the top tourist spots and are a perfect holiday destination for nature lovers. The Indian Islands are rich with green landscape and beautiful beaches, and are well known for water sport activities like diving, rafting and snorkeling facilities. These islands are basically the treasured assets that Mother Nature has bestowed on us. These islands demonstrate a splendid beauty and impressive locales.

The Andaman and Nicobar Islands is a union territory of India. This Union Territory is stretched over an area of more than 700 km. from north to south with 36 inhabited islands. The Islands consist of 2 groups, the Andaman and Nicobar. The capital city of these islands is *Port Blair.* Of the total land area, 92% of the land is covered with rainforests. Of the 527 islands, in only 38 islands we find the inhabitants. The rest of the land is barren.The Nicobar Islands are inhabited by the backward communities and primitive tribes. The people in the islands speak many languages. The ideal time to visit this island is from December to March. The place has abundance of natural beauty to look forward to.

The Lakshadweep is the smallest union territory of India. Lakshadweep is the northern part of the former Lakshadweepa. It consists of 12 atolls, 3 reefs and 5 submerged banks. The atolls poised on the submarine banks, harbour 36 islands having an area of 32 sq. km. of these, only 10 islands are inhabited. The main languages spoken in Lakshadweep are Malayalam and Mahl. Lakshadweep is under the jurisdiction of the High Court of Kerala at Ernakulam. Nowadays, Lakshadweep is emerging as a major tourist attraction for Indians. This brings in considerable revenue. Since such a small region cannot support industries, the government is actively promoting tourism as a means of income. The Lakshadweep Islands are famous for its exotic locales and environment. The place exhibits abundant natural beauty.

2. River System of India

The river systems in India can be classified into four groups:
⇨ The Himalayan Rivers,
⇨ The Deccan Rivers,
⇨ The Coastal Rivers
⇨ Rivers of the Inland Drainage Basin

The Himalayan rivers are formed by melting snow and glaciers and therefore, continuously flow throughout the year. During the monsoon months, the Himalayas receive very heavy rainfall and rivers swell, causing frequent floods.

The Deccan rivers on the other hand are rainfed and therefore fluctuate in volume. Many of these are non-perennial.

The Coastal streams or rivers, especially on the west coast are short in length and have limited catchment areas. Most of them are non-perennial. The streams of inland drainage basin of western Rajasthan are few and far apart. Most of them are of an ephemeral character.

The main Himalayan river systems are those of the Indus and the Ganga-Brahmaputra-Meghna system.

The Indus, which is one of the great rivers of the world, rises near Mansarovar in Tibet and flows through India and thereafter through Pakistan and finally falls in the Arabian sea near Karachi. Its important tributaries flowing in the Indian territory are the Sutlej (originating in Tibet), the Beas, the Ravi, the Chenab and the Jhelum.

The Ganga-Brahmaputra-Meghna is another important system of which the principal sub-basins are those of Bhagirathi and the Alaknanda, which join at Dev Prayag to form the Ganga. It traverses through Uttarakhand, Uttar Pradesh, Bihar and West Bengal states. Below Rajmahal hills, the Bhagirathi, which used to be the main course in the past, takes off, while the Padma continues eastward and enters Bangladesh. The Yamuna, the

Ramganga, the Ghaghra, the Gandak, the Kosi, the Mahananda and the Sone are the important tributaries of the Ganga. Rivers Chambal and Betwa are the important sub-tributaries, which join Yamuna before it meets the Ganga. The Padma and the Brahmaputra join at Bangladesh and continue to flow as the Padma or Ganga. The Brahmaputra rises in Tibet, where it is known as Tsangpo and runs a long distance till it crosses over into India in Arunachal Pradesh under the name of Dihang. Near Passighat, the Debang and Lohit join the river Brahmaputra and the combined river runs all along the Assam in a narrow valley. It crosses into Bangladesh downstream of Dhubri.

The principal tributaries of Brahmaputra in India are the Subansiri, JiaBhareli, Dhansiri, Puthimari, Pagladiya and the Manas. The Brahmaputra in Bangladesh fed by Tista etc., finally falls into Ganga. The Barak river, the Head stream of Meghna, rises in the hills in Manipur. The important tributaries of the river are Makku, Trang, Tuivai, Jiri, Sonai, Rukni, Katakhal, Dhaleswari, Langachini, Maduva and Jatinga.

In the Deccan region, most of the major river systems flowing generally in east direction fall into Bay of Bengal. The major east flowing rivers are Godavari, Krishna, Cauvery, Mahanadi, etc. Narmada and Tapti are major West flowing rivers.

The Godavari in the southern Peninsula has the second largest river basin covering 10 per cent of the area of India. Next to it is the Krishna basin in the region, while the Mahanadi has the third largest basin.

The basin of the Narmada in the uplands of the Deccan, flowing to the Arabian Sea and of the Kaveri in the south, falling into the Bay of Bengal are about the same size, though with different character and shape.

There are numerous coastal rivers, which are comparatively small. While only handful of such rivers drains into the sea near the delta of east coast, there are as many as 600 such rivers on the west coast.

A few rivers in Rajasthan do not drain into the sea. They drain into salt lakes and get lost in sand with no outlet to sea.

Besides these, there are the Desert Rivers which flow for some distance and are lost in the desert. These are *Luni, Machhu, Rupen, Saraswati, Banas, Ghaggar* and others.

3. Climate

India's climate is varied but is tropical in the south and mainly temperate in the north. The country also has a pronounced monsoon season from June to September in it southern portion.

From the values of latitude, it is understood that the southern part of the country lies within the tropics and the northern part lies in the sub-tropical zone or the warm temperate zone. This location is responsible for the large variations in land forms, climate, soil types and natural vegetation in the country.

The Indian climate can be categorised into six principal subcategories and this has been determined by the Koppen climatic classification.

Name of the season	Tenure
Winter	The months of January and February
Summer	The months of March to May
Monsoon (rainy) season	The months of June to September
A post-monsoon period	The months of October to December

The winter in India spans the months of *December till the beginning of April*. The coldest months of the year are *January and December*. During this period, the average temperature is approximately 50-59°F (10-15°C) in the northwestern parts of the country. The mercury soars as you move in the direction of the equator, and the maximum temperature in this area is close to 68-77°F or 20-25°C in the southeastern parts of the Indian Territory.

The summer months are the months of April to June. However, the summer refers to the months of April to July in the northwestern parts of the country. In the southern and western parts of the country, the month with the maximum recorded temperature is April. In case of the northern parts of the country, the month with the maximum recorded temperature is May. The average temperature registered during these months is close to 90-104°F (32-40°C) in majority of the inland areas of the country.

The monsoon, also known as the rainy season, spans the months of June to September. This season is primarily influenced with the moist southwestern summer torrential rainfall that gradually moves throughout the nation. It starts in the end of May or the beginning of June. The precipitation starts to ebb from Northern India in the early October. Usually, the southern parts of the country get higher volume of precipitation than the northern parts of the country.

The post-monsoon season spans the months of October to December. In the northwest parts of the country, the months of November and October normally have a bright weather. The Indian state of Tamil Nadu gets the maximum volume of yearly rainfall in the northeastern rainy season.

The various climatic regions of India are given below:

Name of the climatic region	States or union territories
Tropical Rainforest	Assam and parts of the Sahyadri Mountain Range
Tropical Savannah	Sahyadri Mountain Range and parts of Maharashtra
Tropical and Subtropical Steppe	Parts of Punjab and Gujarat
Tropical Desert	Most parts of Rajasthan
Moist Subtropical with Winter	Parts of Punjab, Assam and Rajasthan
Mountain Climate	Parts of Jammu and Kashmir, Himachal Pradesh, and Uttarakhand
Drought	Rajasthan, Gujarat and Haryana
Tropical Semi-arid Steppe	Tamil Nadu, Maharashtra and other parts of South India

4. Forests

India houses different types of forests and woodlands. These forests include protected forests or reserved forests. Prior to the independence of the country, the forests were protected under the Indian Forest Act, 1927. Post-Independence, the Indian Government has preserved the status of the prevailing protected and reserved forests of the country.

The forests of India can be broadly categorised into two types –

⇨ Undemarcated protected forests and
⇨ Demarcated protected forests.

This categorisation has been made on the basis that whether the boundaries of the forest have been delineated by an official declaration.

The abundant and varied flora and fauna of India are housed in 13 biosphere reserves, 89 national parks, and more than 400 wildlife sanctuaries located throughout the nation.

The different types of forests of India are classified below:

⇨ Tropical Rainforests
⇨ Temperate Deciduous Forests
⇨ Himalayan Subtropical Pine Forests
⇨ Indian Tidal or Mangrove Forests
⇨ Indian Dry Deciduous Forests
⇨ Humid Deciduous Forests of the Eastern Highlands
⇨ Dry Evergreen Forests of the East Deccan Region
⇨ Monsoon Forests

Approximately 20% of the overall forest cover of India is located in the state of Madhya Pradesh. States like Maharashtra, Odisha, Andhra Pradesh, Uttar Pradesh, and Arunachal Pradesh also house a considerable volume of forests.

The second biggest land use in the country after farming is forests. Forests encompass about 67.83 million hectares of area in India which represents 20.64% of the nation's geographical territory, varying from the arid zone forests to the Himalayan temperate forests.

5. Types of Soils and Agriculture

The Indian Council of Agricultural Research (ICAR) has divided the Indian soils into eight major groups:

⇨ **Alluvial Soil**: This is the largest and the most important soil group of India. They are composed of sediments deposited by rivers and the waves. Their chemical composition makes them one of the most fertile in the world. Fertilizers are generally required because they are deficient in humus and nitrogen. They are found in the plains (from Punjab to Assam) and in the valleys

T-Value of Soils in India

of Narmada and Tapti in Madhya Pradesh and Gujarat, Mahanadi in Madhya Pradesh and Odisha, Godavari in Andhra Pradesh and Cauvery in Tamil Nadu. The Alluvial soil is divided into the following:

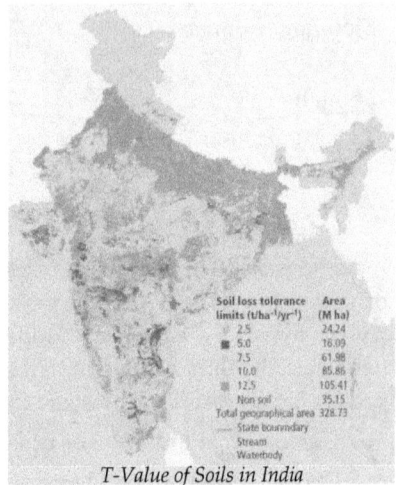

- *Khadar* (new)
- *Bhangar* (old)

⇨ **Black Soil**: It is also called *Regur* and is ideal for cultivating cotton, cereals, oilseeds, citrus fruits and vegetables, tobacco and sugarcane. These soils have been formed from the solidification of lava spread over large areas during volcanic activity in the Deccan Plateau, thousands of years ago. The soil is black due to compounds of iron and aluminium (also because of titaniferous magnetite). They have high moisture retention. They lack in phosphorus, nitrogen and organic matter. It is mainly found in the Deccan Plateau – Maharashtra, Gujarat, Madhaya Pradesh, Karnataka, Andhra Pradesh and Tamil Nadu.

⇨ **Red Soil**: This is mainly formed from the decomposition of ancient crystalline rocks like granites and gneisses and from rock types rich in minerals, such as iron and magnesium. The term, 'red soil' is due to the wide diffusion of iron oxides through the materials of the soil, thus giving it its characteristic red colour. It covers almost the whole of Tamil Nadu, Karnataka, Andhra Pradesh, South-East Maharashtra, Chhattisgarh, parts of Odisha, Jharkhand and Bundelkhand. It is generally deficient in nitrogen, humus and phosphorus, but rich in potash. It is suitable for cultivation of rice, millets, tobacco and vegetables (also groundnuts and potatoes at higher elevations).

➪ **Laterite Soil:** It is found in typical monsoon conditions – conditions of high temperature and heavy rainfall with alternate wet and dry periods. The alterations of wet and dry season leads to the drainage of siliceous matter and lime of the rocks, and then a soil rich in oxides of iron and aluminium compounds is left behind. It is found in parts of Western Ghats, Eastern Ghats, Rajmahal hills, Maharashtra, Karnataka, Kerala, Odisha, West Bengal, Assam, Tamil Nadu, etc. It is poor in nitrogen and minerals. It is the best soil for tea, coffee, rubber, cinchona, coconut and is also suitable for rice and millet cultivation if manure is used.

➪ **Forests and Mountain Soils:** This is mainly found on the hill slopes covered by forests. The formation of these soils is mainly governed by the deposition of organic matter derived from forest growth.In the Himalayan region, such soils are mainly found in valley basins, depressions and less steeply inclined slopes. Apart from the Himalayan region, the forest soils occur in higher hills in south and the peninsular region. These are very rich in humus but are deficient in Potash, phosphorous and lime and need fertilizers. They are suitable for plantation of tea, coffee, spices and tropical fruits.

➪ **Arid and Desert Soils:** A large part of the arid and semi-arid region in Rajasthan and adjoining areas of Punjab and Haryana receiving less than 50 cm of annual rainfall is affected by desert conditions. This area is covered by a blanket of sand which restricts soil growth.The phosphate content of these soils is as high as in normal alluvial soils. Nitrogen is originally low but its deficiency is made up to some extent by the availability of nitrogen in the form of nitrates. Thus the presence of phosphates and nitrates make them fertile soils wherever moisture is available.The changes in the cropping pattern in the Indira Gandhi Canal Command Area are an amazing example of the utility of the desert soils.

➪ **Saline and Alkaline Soils: They are** found in the drier parts of Bihar, Uttar Pradesh, Haryana, Punjab, Rajasthan and Maharshtra. They are known by different names, such as Reh, Kallar, USAR, etc. Some of the salts are transported in solution by the rivers and canals, which percolates in the sub-soils of the plains. The accumulation of salts makes the soil infertile thereby making it unfit for agriculture.

⇨ **Peaty and Marshy Soils:** They originate in humid regions due of accumulation of large amounts of organic matter in the soil. They contain considerable amounts of soluble salts and 10–40% of organic matter. Marshy soils are high in vegetable matter. Peaty soils are found in Kottayam and Alappuzha districts of Kerala, where it is called **Kari**. The Marshy soils are found in northern Bihar, coastal parts of Odisha, Tamil Nadu and West Bengal and parts of Uttar Pradesh.

Agriculture

India is majorly an agriculture-based country where about 60-70 percent people depend on it and about 50 percent (approx.. 142.42 million hectares) of total land is under cultivation.

The major crop seasons in India are:

⇨ **Kharif:** Crops are sown at the beginning of the south-west monsoon and harvested at the end of the south-west monsoon.
  ▪ Sowing seasons-May to July
  ▪ Harvesting season-September to October
  ▪ Important crops: Jowar, bajra, rice, maize, cotton, groundnut, jute, hemp, sugarcane, tobacco, etc.

⇨ **Rabi:** Crops need relatively cool climate during the period of growth and warm climate during the germination and maturation.
  ▪ Sowing season-October to December
  ▪ Harvesting season-February to April
  ▪ Important crops: wheat, barley, gram, linseed, mustard, masoor, pea and potatoes.

⇨ **Zaid:** Besides the kharif and rabi crops, there are certain crops which are cultivated throughout the year with artificial irrigation.

⇨ **Zaid-kharif** crops are sown in August-September and harvested in December-January.
  ▪ Important crops: rice, jowar, rapeseed, cotton, oilseeds.

⇨ **Zaid-rabi** crops are sown in February-March and harvested in April-May.
  ▪ Important crops: watermelon, tori, cucumber, leafy and other vegetables.

6. Landmarks in Indian Agriculture

Green Revolution: This movement was launched in 1967-1968 in a bid to increase agricultural output. The purpose was to make India self-sufficient in food grains, with the introduction of High-Yielding Varieties

(HYVs) of seeds and increased use of fertilizers and irrigation, thereby increasing and improving the agricultural output. Genetically modified high-yielding *wheat* was first introduced in India in 1963 by *Dr. Norman Borlaug*.

The idea of agricultural revolution was taken further ahead by the enthusiasm shown by farmers. *M. S. Swaminathan, 'The Father of the Green Revolution in India'* and his team were credited for having contributed to the success of the Green Revolution. Wheat production doubled and rice production increased by 53%.

However, land and soil resources were highly degraded because of the rise in the use of chemical pesticides and fertilizers.

The First Green Revolution occurred mainly in Punjab, Haryana and Uttar Pradesh. The Second Green Revolution took place in 1983-84 in the eastern states of Odisha, Bihar, Madhya Pradesh and the eastern part of Uttar Pradesh.

Operation Flood: This operation was a rural development programme started by India's National Dairy Development Board (NDDB) in 1970, in collaboration with the World Bank. The main aim of this programme was to increase the milk market in urban areas.

Operation Flood's objectives included:
➪ Increase milk production ("a flood of milk")
➪ Augment rural incomes
➪ Fair prices for consumers

Phase II (1981) extended the programme to all states. Phase III (1985-90) was launched in 1985 during the seventh five year plan.

Gujarat-based cooperation "the Anand Milk Union Limited", better known as Amul, was the agent of this programme's success. Tribhuvandas Patel was the founder Chairman of Amul, while Verghese Kurien was the chairman of NDDB at the time when the programme was implemented. Kurien is considered the architect of India's 'White Revolution' (Operation Flood).

The operation was a huge success and managed to make India the second largest producer of milk. It helped in reducing malpractices by milk traders and merchants.

Irrigation and Agriculture
India's agriculture mostly depends on rains because of its climatic location. However, even rain water is not sufficient and other methods are required to provide water to crops. Irrigation is a method of providing water to dry lands by means of ditches, wells etc.

Methods of Irrigation

Wells: These account for about 47% of the total irrigated land and are used in Uttar Pradesh, Punjab, Tamil Nadu and Maharashtra.

Tanks: These provide water to around 10% of the total area. They are mainly used in Central and Southern India.

Canals: These are spread over 40% of the total area. They are used in Uttar Pradesh, Punjab, Haryana and Odisha, which has presently become 'Odisha'.

7. Mineral Resources in India

India is a rich source of mineral. A variety of minerals is spread over the country. Some important minerals that are available here are:

⇨ **Iron**
   Found in Odisha, Bihar, Jharkhand, Andhra Pradesh, Tamil Nadu, Karnataka, Maharashtra, and Goa.
   India has the world's largest reserve of iron.

⇨ **Coal**
   Good reserves of coal are found in Bihar, West Bengal, Odisha, Madhya Pradesh, Maharashtra, Andhra Pradesh and Assam.
   India is the third largest producer of coal.

⇨ **Manganese**
   Found in Odisha, Madhya Pradesh, Maharashtra, Gujarat, Karnataka, Jharkhand, Andhra Pradesh.
   India is the third largest producer of manganese.

⇨ **Mica**
   Found in Jharkhand, Rajasthan, Andhra Pradesh, Tamil Nadu.
   India has the largest reserves of mica in the world.

⇨ **Bauxite** (Aluminium ore)
   Found in Jharkhand, Gujarat, Chhattisgarh, Tamil Nadu, Karnataka, Maharashtra, Jammu & Kashmir, Odisha.
   India is the third largest producer of bauxite.

⇨ **Crude Oil**
   Found in Assam, Tripura, Manipur, West Bengal, Himachal Pradesh, Kutch, Maharashtra and Gujarat.

⇨ **Gold**
   Found in Karnataka and Andhra Pradesh.

⇨ **Gypsum**
   Rajasthan, Jammu & Kashmir and Tamil Nadu.

8. National Parks and Wildlife Sanctuaries

India is a country with a diverse beautiful wildlife spread all across the country. The protection of this wildlife is very important in today's world. There are several national parks and sanctuaries for this job.

East India

➪ **Sunderbans National Park**

Located in the Ganga delta in West Bengal, spanning the Hooghly in the west and Teulia river in the east, Sunderbans was declared a National Park in 1984. The park covers a vast stretch of mangrove swamp, lush forested islands and small rivers near the Bay of Bengal. Most of the region comprises estuarine mangrove forests and swamps which supports an ecosystem specially adapted to great salinity.

■ **Fauna**

Sundarbans is a home to the magnificent Royal Bengal tiger, the park holding more tigers than any other tiger reserve. More than 400 tigers were recorded during the mid-1980s. The Project, Tiger has also launched a programme to protect the Olive Ridley sea turtles. Crocodiles and the gangetic dolphin are to be found plenty in the Raimgangal river. The Sajnakhali Sanctuary, famous for in its rich avian population, is regarded as a part of the Sunderbans National Park.

➪ **Ambapani Sanctuary**

Located 77-kms from Bhawanipatna and 45 kms from Nowrangpur, Ambapani is famous for the deity of Budharaja installed in a small temple at the foot of a hill. The picturesque Ambapani hills present a panoramic view of nature. A frolicking valley called Haladigundi in this range of hills exhibits some peculiar features due to the reflected rays of the sun.

■ **Fauna**

The whole area abounds in Spotted Deer, Sambar and Black Panthers, which can be seen at the Behera reservoir. Situated 5-kms away are the pre-historic cave paintings at Gudahandi.

➪ **Kaziranga National Park**

It lies on the south bank of the Brahmaputra and its boundary for the most part follows the Mora Diphlu river and runs parallel to the National Highway No. 37. It covers an area of about 688 sq. km. The Park was first established in 1908, as a reserve forest with only about a dozen rhinos and was declared a National Park in 1974.

■ **Flora and Fauna**

The Kaziranga is famous for the great one-horned Rhinos. Tigers which are natural enemies of rhinos are also there in sizable numbers in this area. Other the attractions of this national park include the wild buffalo, magnificent swamp deer, hog deer, wild boar, Hoolok gibbon, capped langur and ratel (badger).

A wide variety of snakes including the rock python and the monitor lizards are also found here. Amongst the birds, the crested serpent eagle is common while palla's fishing eagle and grey headed fishing eagle are frequently seen. Others include the Bengal floricab, bar-headed goose, whistling teal and pelican.

West India

⇨ **Nalsarovar Bird Sanctuary**

Just 65 kms southwest of Ahmedabad, is the delightful bird sanctuary of Nalsarovar nestling around the Nal Lake, extending over 11,500 hectares. Established in 1969 AD, it is known to harbour over 250 species of wetland birds.

■ **The Inhabitants and the Visitors**

Nalsarovar sees winter migrants from the north that include rosy pelicans, flamingoes, white storks, brahminy ducks and herons. The Nalsarovar Bird Sanctuary is one of the best of its kind in India during the winter months, teeming with thousands of cranes, flamingoes, pelicans, ducks, storks and other birds. The jungle cat, the jackal and the hare can also be seen here.

■ **Bird Watching**

A pair of binoculars and a person well versed in the local bird life will surely make it one of your best outings. Visitors are ferried in small boats to experience a sunrise or sunset while gliding gently through the silent waters. Country boats of the local people are available for birdwatching on the lake.

⇨ **Tansa Wildlife Sanctuary**

The Tansa Wildlife Sanctuary is located in Wada, Shahapur and the MokhadaTalukas of Thane district. The wildlife sanctuary at Tansa comprises the catchment area of Tansa Lake and the surrounding forests of Shahapur, Khardi, Vaitarna and East Wada Ranges in Shahapur Tehsil of Thana district. The Tansa Lake is a perennial source of water to wildlife in the sanctuary.

■ **Flora**

The land vegetation is southern tropical moist deciduous forest. The major tree species found in this area are Teak, Khair, Ain, Hed, Kalamb, Bibla, etc. Bamboo is also spotted in small patches over here.

- **Fauna**

  This Wildlife Sanctuary hosts a wide range of species. There are around 50 species of animals and about 200 bird species in this area. Major wild animals are Panther, Barking Deer, Mouse Deer, Hyena, Wild boar, Leopard, Jackal, Four-Horned Antelope, Chital, Sambar, Hare, Common Langur, etc.

▷ **Nayagaon Mayur Sanctuary**

The sanctuary is located in the hilly forest areas of villages in Patoda Taluka of Beed District in the Marathwada region. The turf of the forest area is hilly in the central plateau region.

- **Flora**

  The patches of scrub forest, plantation blocks, grasslands and blanks are scattered throughout the area. The forest vegetation includes stunted growth of Chinch, Jamun, Sitafal, Tendu, Neem, Sandalwood, Ficus Species, etc. The major shrubs that grow over here are Lantana, Karwand, Bor, Lokhandi, etc. The plantation area of the sanctuary has thickets of Glyricidia.

- **Fauna**

  The major animals that are spotted by the tourists are Wolf, Fox, Hyena, Black Buck Porcupine, Palm Civet, Jungle Cat, Hare, etc. Pea Fowls are seen in much larger numbers all over the area.

▷ **Ranthambhore National Park**

Near the township of Sawai Madhopur, in the state of Rajasthan, the Ranthambore National Park is an outstanding example of *Project Tiger's* efforts at the conservation of forests in the country. The forests around the Ranthambore Fort were once, the private hunting grounds of the Maharajas of Jaipur. The desire to preserve the game in these forests for sport, was responsible for their conservation, and subsequent rescue by the Project Tiger.

The Park sprawls over an estimated area of 400 sq kms. Steep crags embracea network of lakes and rivers, and a top one of these hills, is the impressive Ranthambore Fort, built in the 10th century. The terrain fluctuates between impregnable forests and open bushland. The forest is the typically dry deciduous type, with dhok, being the most prominent tree. The entry point to the Park, goes straight to the foot of the fort and the forest rest house, Jogi Mahal. The latter boasts of the second-largest banyan tree in India.

The Padam Talab, the Raj Bagh Talab and the Milak Talab are some of the lakes in the area, that attract the tiger population . They have been spotted at the edges of these lakes, and JogiMahal itself. Old crumbling walls, ruined pavilions, wells, and other ancient structures stand witness to the region's glorious past.

The entire forest is peppered with the battlements and spillovers of the Ranthambore Fort - tigers are said to frequent these ruins, too. As a result of stringent efforts in conservation, tigers, the prime assets of the Park, have become more and more active during the day. More than in any other park or sanctuary in India, tigers are easily spotted here in daylight. They can be seen lolling around lazily in the sun, or feverishly hunting down sambar around the lakes.

⇨ **Sariska National Park**

Sariska became a sanctuary in the year 1958. The sanctuary came under the Project Tiger in 1979 and became a national park in 1982. It is located at Kankwari Fort, near Alwar, on the Delhi Jaipur Highway. The terrain is predominantly hilly, as it lies in the Aravalli range. It has total area of 788 sq.kms, with a core area of approximately 47 sq.kms.

■ **Fauna**

At the last count in 1985, there were 35 tigers reported. Other carnivores of the area are the panther, jungle cat, jackal and hyena. Three caracals were also reported during the last census in 1985. Other animals include the sambhar, chital, wild boar, hare, nilgai and umpteen porcupines.

⇨ **Corbett National Park**

The Corbett National Park is located in the terai region of the state of Uttar Pradesh, straddling the undulating Shivalik foothills of the Himalayas. Located around 300 kilometres away from New Delhi, it is *India's first ever national park*. The park was established in 1936 as the Hailey National Park, following the advice of the hunter-naturalist Jim Corbett. The park covered 520 sq.kms in 1986, and a proposed extension of 588 sq.kms is under consideration.

The Project Tiger, which was set up with the help of the World Wildlife Fund, was launched at Dhikala, in the Corbett National Park on April 1, 1973. This project was aimed at saving the Indian tiger (Panthera tigris tigris) from extinction. Over 50 mammals, 580 birds and 25 reptile species have been listed in the Corbett National Park. The insect life is also astounding, noticeably specially after the monsoons. But undoubtedly, the jewel of the Corbettis the Indian tiger. It was estimated that in 1984, the tiger population was 90 in this park. Leopards as well as lesser cats such as the leopard cat, jungle cat, fishing cat are also found here.

- **Fauna**

  The sloth bear, Himalayan black bear, dhole, jackal, yellow throated martem, Himalyan palm civet, Indian greymongoose, common otter, porcupine, clacktaped hare are the other attractions of this area. It is possible to see elephants all over the park. Four species of deer are found here. These are the chital, the well-known spotted deer, para, kakka, and the barking deer. The goat antelopes are represented by the ghoral. There is a lot for the bird watchers in this park. It has over 580 species of birds. Most of the water birds are migrant, and arrive in winters. Some of these are the greylag, barheaded goose, duck, grepe, snipe, sand piper, gull and wagtail. The residents include darters, cormorants, egrets, herons, the blacknecked stork and the spurwinged lapwings. Reptiles, which are residents of this area, are the gharial, the rare fish eating, long - nosed crocodile, and a few species of turtlesand tortoises.

  The Indian python, viper, cobra, krait and kingcobra also inhabit the Corbett National Park. The National Park offers invaluable experiences for adventurous and serious-minded wildlife - buffs, photographers and anglers. It is advantageous to have one's own vehicle here. Walking in some areas is permitted, but only when accompanied by a guide. Elephant rides for wildlife viewing, in the mornings and evenings, can be booked in the Dhikala complex.

South India

⇨ **Kalkadu Wildlife Sanctuary**

The Kalakadu Wildlife Sanctuary is situated in an area of 223-sq-kms in the Tirunelveli district, including the foothills of the Western Ghats and the adjoining areas. 47-kms from Tirunelveli, the Kalakadu Wildlife Sanctuary is very popular with botanists and ornithologists as it has a great variety of fauna and bird life.

- **Flora**

  The flora ranges from the forests of Tropical Wet Evergreen to Tropical Dry Deciduous and Thorn Forests at down hills.

- **Fauna**

  It is a Lion tailed Macaque's preserve. The Lion tailed Macaque, Nilgiri Langur, Bonnet Macaque, Common Langur, Nilgiri Tahr, Sambar, Sloth Bear, Gaur, Elephant, Tiger, Flying Squirrel, Panther, Wild Dog, Pangoline are some of the wildlife seen in the sanctuary.

⇨ **Periyar National Park**

Between Trivandrum and Munnar is Thekkady, the home of one of

India's oldest and best-known wildlife sancturies, the former princely state of Travancore began to develop the area as a sanctuary in 1934, using the artificial lake that had been formed by flooding in 1895 as its centre, by 1950 the sanctuary had reached its present size of 780 square kilometres and was named as the Periyar Wildlife Sanctuary.

The sanctuary is in fact closer to Madurai in Tamil Nadu, 140 kilometres to the east via an extremely attractive road, and Cochin, 200 kilometres to the west. The vast calmness of the lake and the stark, skeletal remains of the trees that protrude from its waters give the area a primeval look. This impression is heightened by the mists that swirl ethereally over the water in the early morning.

- **Fauna**

  The wildlife remains largely undisturbed by visitors who must observe it from special boats which glide across the surface of the lake. Although the stars of the sanctuary are the families of wild elephants that often gather near the water's edge, other inhabitants include bears, sambhar, bison and spotted deer, as well as many screeching monkeys. The sanctuary was one of the first to come under the Central government's successful Project Tiger. The birdlife is rich and varied and Periyar attracts dedicated bird-watching enthusiasts.

▷ **Srisailam Sanctuary**

Just near to this sanctuary is the reservoir of the Nagarjunasagar Dam on the Krishna river. This is the country's largest tiger reserves. This Srisailam sanctuary is spread over an area of 3568 sq.km.

- **The Flora and Fauna**

  Dry deciduous mixed forest with scrub and bamboo thickets provide shelter to a wide range of animals. The terrain is rugged and winding gorges slice through the Nallamalai hills. Spotted Deers, Mouse Deers, Black Bucks, Sambhars, Chousingha, Nilgai, Wild Boars, Indian Giant Squirrels, Tree Shrews, Rayels, Mugger Crocodiles, Wild Dogs, Jackals, Wolves, Foxes, Sloth Bear, Panthers and Tigers are the animal attractions of this sanctuary.

  In this forest, the tiger is truly nocturnal and is rarely seen. The reserve was a home to about 100 tigers at the beginning of this decade. However, according to a census conducted in 1997, the tiger population has fallen steeply to about 20.

9. Indian States and Union Territories

India is a federal union comprising *twenty eight states* and *seven union territories*. The capital is *New Delhi*.

List of States

Andhra Pradesh	Arunachal Pradesh	Assam
Bihar	Chhattisgarh	Goa
Gujarat	Haryana	Himachal Pradesh
Jammu and Kashmir	Jharkhand	Karnataka
Kerala	Madhya Pradesh	Maharashtra
Manipur	Meghalaya	Mizoram
Nagaland	Odisha	Punjab
Rajasthan	Sikkim	Tamil Nadu
Tripura	Uttarakhand	Uttar Pradesh
West Bengal		

List of Union Territories

Andaman and Nicobar Islands	Daman and Diu
Chandigarh	Lakshadweep
The Government of NCT of Delhi	Pondicherry or Puducherry
Dadra and Nagar Haveli	

10. Demography/Census/Language/Literacy/Sex Ratio

India is the second most populous country in the world, with a population of over 1.21 billion according to the 2011 census. It is predicted that the country will surpass China by 2025 to become the world's most populated country, and it is believed that its population will reach 1.6 billion by 2050. Its population growth rate is 1.41 percent.

The Census 2001, the fifteenth since 1872, showed that at 0.00 hours on 1st March 2011, India's population stood at 1,21,01,93,422 with an increase of 17.64 percent since the last census in 2001.

The Census was carried out in two phases, with an estimated 2.7 million officials being used to help with the job of creating a database on demography, economic activity, literacy and education, housing and household amenities, urbanisation, fertility and morality, social structure, language, religion and migration.

(Census : 2011)

Population	Total	1,210,193,422
	Males	623,724,248
	Females	586,469,174
Literacy	Total	74.04%
	Males	82.14%
	Females	65.46%
Density of Population	per km^2	382
Sex Ratio	per 1000 males	940 females
Child Sex Ratio (0–6 age group)	per 1000 males	914 females

Sex Ratio

At birth	1.12 male(s)/female (2009 est.)
Under 15	1.10 male(s)/female (2009 est.)
15-64 years	1.06 male(s)/female (2009 est.)
65-over	0.90 male(s)/female (2009 est.)

Language

The various languages of India are derived from a number of language families. The dominant ones are the Indo-Aryan languages, spoken by 74 percent Indians, and Dravidian languages, spoken by 24 percent. Other languages belong to the Austro-Asiatic, Tibeto-Burman, and a few other minor language families.

The official language of India is Hindi (in Devanagari Script), while English is the second official language. Individual mother tongues in India go upto several hundred. According to the Census of 2001, 30 languages are spoken by more than a million native speakers, 122 by more than 10,000.

11. Important Towns and Locations

Prominent Indian Cities on River Banks

City	River	State
Agra	Yamuna	Uttar Pradesh
Ahmedabad	Sabarmati	Gujarat
Allahabad	Confluence of the Ganges, Yamuna and Saraswati	Uttar Pradesh
Alwaye	Periyar	Kerala

Ayodhya	Sarayu	Uttar Pradesh
Badrinath	Gangotri	Uttarakhand
Bhagalpur	Ganges	Bihar
Buxar	Ganges	Bihar
Kolkata	Hooghly	West Bengal
Cuttack	Mahanadi	Odisha
Delhi	Yamuna	Delhi
Dibrugarh	Brahmaputra	Assam
Guwahati	Brahmaputra	Assam
Haridwar	Ganges	Uttarakhand
Howrah	Hooghly	West Bengal
Hyderabad	Musa	Andhra Pradesh
Jamshedpur	Subarnarekha	Jharkhand
Kanpur	Ganges	Uttar Pradesh
Kota	Chambal	Rajasthan
Leh	Indus	Jammu and Kashmir
Lucknow	Gomti	Uttar Pradesh
Ludhiana	Sutlej	Punjab
Mathura	Yamuna	Utter Pradesh
Moradabad	Ram Ganga	Uttar Pradesh
Monghyr	Ganges	Uttar Pradesh
Nashik	Godavari	Maharashtra
Patna	Ganges/Sone	Bihar
Srinagar	Jhelum	Jammu and Kashmir
Surat	Tapti	Gujarat
Tiruchirappalli	Cauvery	Tamil Nadu
Ujjain	Shipra	Madhya Pradesh
Vijayawada	Krishna	Andhra Pradesh
Varanasi	Ganges	Uttar Pradesh

12. Important Sites and Monuments

Name	Location	Famour for
Ajanta Caves	Aurangabad	Buddhist cave temples
Amarnath's cave	Kashmir	Natrullay formed ice Shivlinga
Anand Bhawan	Allahabad	Ancestral house of the Nehru family which has been donated by Late Mrs Indira Gandhi for conversion into a national Museum.
Bibi-ka-Makbara	Aurangabad	According to the Arachaeological Survey of India, the Bibi-ka-Maqbara is a mausoleum of Rabia-ul-Daurani alias Dilras Baini Begum, the wife of the Mughal Emperor Aurangzeb. This mausoleum is believed to be constructed by Prince Azam Shah in memory of his mother during 1651 to 1661 AD.
Buland Darwaza	Fatehpur Sikri	The highest and biggest gateway of India near Agra built by Akbar to commemorate his victorious campaign in Deccan
Char Minar	Hyderabad	
Dilwara Temples	Mount Abu	Jain temples. Vimal Vasahi, Luna Vasahi. Pittdhar. Parsuvanattra. Mahavir Swami, built between llih and 13 century AD
Elephanta Caves	Mumbai	The Elephanta caves, taluka Uran, district Raigad. is located on island hills, 7 kms from the mainland Mumbai, known for sculptures
Ellora Caves	Aurangabad	Has 12 Buddhist caves. 17 Hindu caves and 5 Jain caves
Gandhi Sadan	Delhi	Birla house—where Gandhiji was assassinated in
Gateway of India	Mumbai	Erected in 1911 on King George V's visit to India
Gol Gumbaz	Bijapur	Largest dome in India

Gomteshwara	Mysore	2000 year-old statue of a Jain sage carved out of a single stone
Golden Temple	Amritsar	Largest Gurudwara
Hawa Mahal	Jaipur	A pink castle of air
Jallianwala Bagh	Amritsar	A public garden infamous for the massacre of hundreds of innocent Indians by the British on 13 April 1919
Jantar Manar	Delhi	Observatory built in 1724 during the days of Maharaja Jai Singh II of Aimer
Jama Masjid	Delhi	Biggest mosque built by Shah Jahan
Kanyakumari	Tamil Nadu	Temple of the Virgin Goddess situated al Cape Camorin on the extreme southern lip of India
Kranti Maidan	Mumbai	Historical avenue where Gandhiji gave the call 'Quit India', in 1942
Khajuraho	Near Bhopal	Mahadeva temple, the embodiment of the great artistic activity of 9th to 12th centuries
Meenakshi Temple	Madurai	Hindu temple
Qutub Minar	Delhi	Largest minaret
Rajghat	Delhi	Samadhi of Mahatma Gandhi on the bank of the Yamuna
Red Fort	Delhi	A red stone structure built by Shah Jahan on the bank of the Yamuna
Sabarmati	Ahmedabad	Harijan Ashram founded here by Gandhiji
Sarnath	Varanasi	Centre of Buddhist pilgrimage, the place where Gautam Buddha delivered his first sermon after enlightenment
Shaktisthal	Delhi	Situated on the bank of the Yamuna where Mrs Indira Gandhi was cremated
Shantivan	Delhi	Samadhi of Pt. Jawaharlal Nehru

Shantiniketan	Kolkata	Famous university founded by Rabindranath Tagore
Sanchi	Madhya Pradesh	Ancient Buddhist monuments
Tower of Victory	Chittorgarh	Famous tower built by Rana Sangha, the king of Mewar, in ad 1450 to commemorate his victory over the Muslim forces of Malwa
Victoria Memorial	Kolkata	Famous museum
Vijay Ghat	Delhi	Samadhi of Lal Bahadur Shastri
Vir Bhumi	Delhi	Samadhi of Rajiv Gandhi

www.ingramcontent.com/pod-product-compliance
Lightning Source LLC
LaVergne TN
LVHW051809080426
835513LV00017B/1879